Baking
Is
Fun
Volume 5

Recipes 351-433

Cover Recipe Page 26

ISBN 0-9691357-4-2

Printed and Bound in Canada

Dear Reader,

The latest volume in the "Baking is Fun" series is dedicated to a very special topic, namely, the many ways of baking with yeast.

Recipes requiring the use of yeast are part of the traditional, classical Austrian kitchen and have, in many cases, been passed on through generations of mothers and grandmothers as true "secrets of the kitchen". They have always been the pride and joy of a good cook and rightly so, for, to be able to successfully produce a yeast cake used to be the sign of a good "Hausfrau".

Today, in our modern, progressive times, among many other formerly difficult tasks, even baking with yeast has lost its problems. The specially treated **oetker** instant dry yeast turns even the novice cook into an expert when using the proper basic recipes.

For this reason we have collected in the beginning of this volume several basic recipes which are the start of many delicious tempting creations. You will also discover many new ideas for delicate cakes and cookies, pastries and savoury treats, as well as yeast cake baking for special occasions. We also present again a number of specially chosen recipes for a variety of tempting bread types. Many of the ideas shown may inspire your imagination and enrich and enhance your weekly meal plan.

As always, all recipes have been carefully chosen and thoroughly tested to guarantee success every time. And, as always, we welcome your ideas and suggestions.

We will certainly be very happy to help complete your "Baking Is Fun" collection, should you be missing any of the previous volumes.

Happy Baking!

oetker ltd

The following baking books are also available:
Baking Is Fun Volume 1, Recipes 1-93
Baking Is Fun Volume 2, Recipes 94-190
Baking Is Fun Volume 3, Recipes 191-270
Baking Is Fun Volume 4, Recipes 271-350

You may order each of these books from

oetker Recipe Service
2229 Drew Road
Mississauga, Ontario
L5S 1E5

Contents

BASIC RECIPES

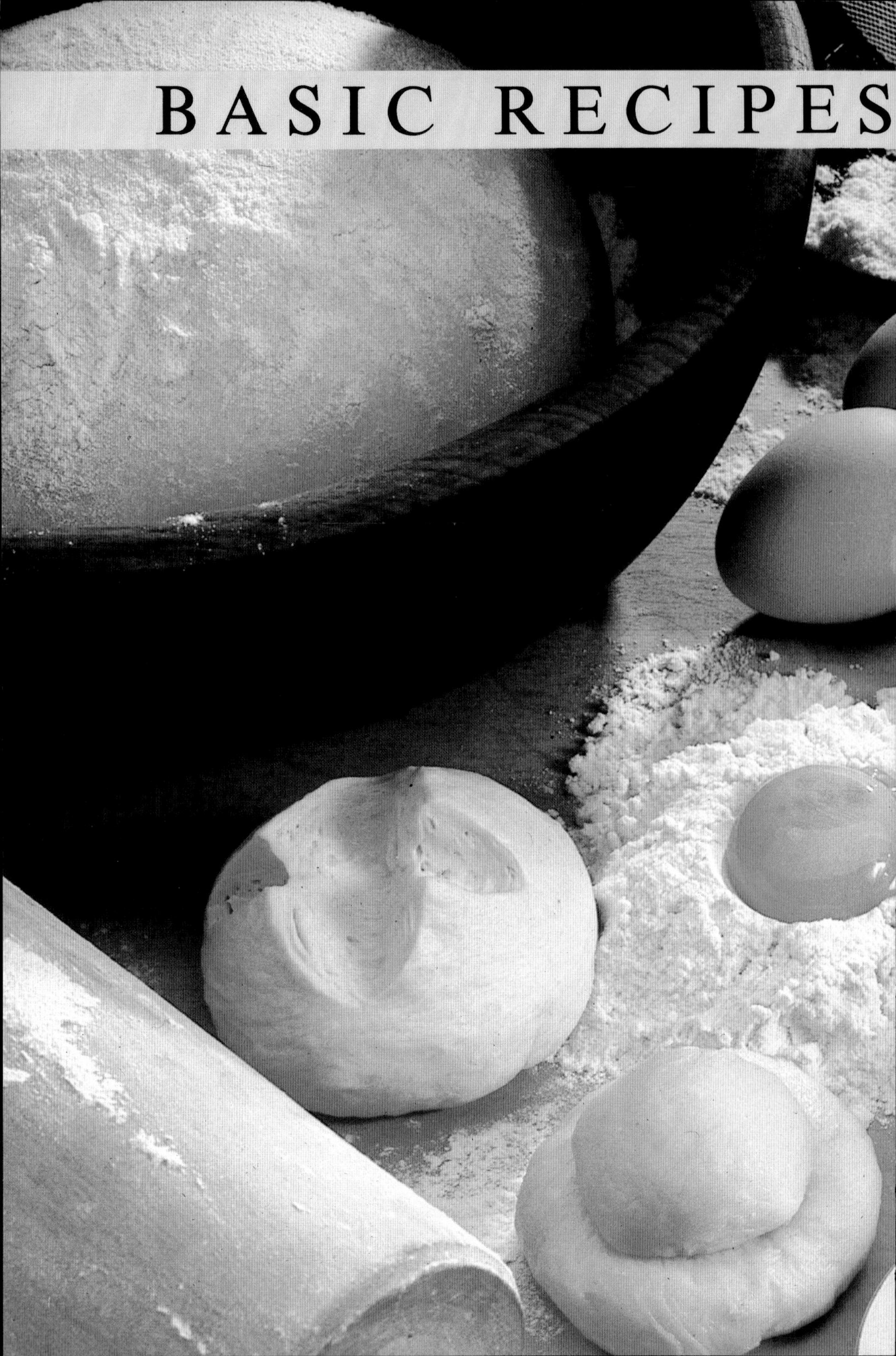

Yeast Dough (Basic Recipe)

In the past baking with yeast was known to be a complicated task. Using **oetker** instant yeast and a little general knowledge about yeast, it almost becomes "child's play" and success is guaranteed every time.

In order to obtain maximum rising power of the yeast, it must be fresh. **oetker** instant dry yeast – through a special process – remains fresh and at optimum quality for up to 18 months in an airtight foil pouch.

Another requirement for continued success is correct temperature of the ingredients and an even room temperature (20-22°C / 68-71°F). For this reason, it is important to have ingredients at room temperature several hours before use and to measure them correctly. If they are too cold, the yeast cannot develop to its fullest potential; if they are too hot, the yeast will die.

Preparation of the dough is very simple. Just mix the flour and **oetker** instant dry yeast well together; add the remaining ingredients and knead with electric dough hooks or by hand until the dough is smooth, elastic and no longer sticky. Kneading takes about 5 minutes.

Before letting dough rise, sprinkle lightly with flour. This will prevent the dough from becoming hard and forming a crust. Cover with a cloth so that heat does not escape from the mixing bowl. Keep dough away from any draft and allow it to rise until doubled in size. Time required to achieve this depends on room temperature.

When rolling out dough (wooden board is better than marble), do not use too much additional flour. This will toughen the dough.

Add fruit always at the end, otherwise dough will be discoloured.

After shaping, allow dough to rise again, covered and in a warm place, to double its size.

Baking pans or sheets should be well greased and sprinkled lightly with flour.

After baking, remove bread immediately from baking pan and place on rack to cool.

By simply observing the following guidelines you can enjoy the taste of freshly baked yeast products at any time.

A yeast dough can be kept in the refrigerator for one day and – depending on fat content – for up to five months in the freezer.

FREEZE baked yeast products when lukewarm – LET THAW at room temperature, then place in hot oven for a few minutes to refreshen.

Dough:

500 g	all-purpose flour	3½	cups
1 pkg	**oetker** instant dry yeast	1	pkg.
50 g	sugar	¼	cup
1 pkg	**oetker** vanilla sugar	1	pkg.
pinch	salt		pinch
½ btl	**oetker** lemon flavouring concentrate	½	btl.
2	eggs	2	
100 g	melted butter or margarine	½	cup
approx 175 mL	lukewarm milk	¾	cup

1. COMBINE flour and **oetker** instant dry yeast in large mixing bowl. Mix well. Make a well in centre.

2. PUT sugar, **oetker** vanilla sugar, salt, **oetker** flavouring concentrate, eggs and melted butter into centre.

3. WORK flour into centre ingredients, gradually adding milk.

4. KNEAD dough with dough hooks or by hand until smooth, elastic and no longer sticky, about 5 minutes.

5. COVER with a cloth. Let dough rise in warm place until doubled in size, about 1¼ hours.

6. PUNCH dough down, shape as directed in individual recipe.

Pastry Dough (Basic Recipe)

oetker instant yeast produces excellent dough for plain, fancy and filled yeast pastries.

Making the dough is very simple and very much like a non-yeast pastry dough. It is important to work quickly and with cold hands (rinse in **cold** water), otherwise the dough will become sticky.

If the dough is too soft, refrigerate it for a few minutes instead of adding more flour which would produce a very tough dough.

By letting the dough rise in the refrigerator, the yeast can only develop slowly. This allows for easy shaping of the dough. Also it will not rise too much during baking.

Sprinkling bread crumbs or ground nuts on the pastry bottom before covering it with a juicy filling or fruit will prevent the dough from becoming soggy. The pastry will retain its crisp texture.

After baking, remove pastry immediately from baking pan and place on rack to cool. This will also prevent the dough from becoming soggy.

Of course, freshly baked pastries always taste best! Eat and enjoy!

Dough:

200 g	all-purpose flour	1⅓	cups
½ pkg	**oetker** instant dry yeast	½	pkg.
		(1½	tsp.)
30 g	sugar	2	tbsp.
1 pkg	**oetker** vanilla sugar	1	pkg.
pinch	salt		pinch
5 drops	**oetker** lemon flavouring concentrate	5	drops
1	egg	1	
100 g	butter or margarine, cold	½	cup

1. Sift flour.

2. COMBINE flour and **oetker** instant dry yeast in large bowl. Make a well in centre.

3. PUT sugar, vanilla sugar, salt, **oetker** flavouring concentrate and egg in centre.

4. COVER with part of the flour; mix thoroughly. CUT cold butter in small pieces over flour mixture.

5. Working quickly from the centre, work all ingredients together. Knead lightly with hands to make a smooth dough.

6. CHILL covered dough for about 1 hour. Knead dough again lightly to allow yeast to "breathe". Chill for another hour before continuing with chosen recipe.

Puff Pastry (Basic Recipe)

Special to this dough is the consistency of the yeast dough and the delicacy of puff pastry.

Since this dough can be frozen, preparation of a larger amount is worthwhile, as the process is rather elaborate.

The basis of this dough is formed by a yeast dough into which butter is worked in layer by layer. Neither the dough nor the butter must be too soft or too hard. If the dough is too soft, it will combine itself with the butter and thereby prevent forming of layers. If the butter is too hard, it cannot be rolled out and will break the dough. Ideally, dough and butter should have the same consistency.

When working the butter into the dough, the dough must be rolled out from the top down and from left to right to achieve even distribution of the butter.

To prevent the dough from sticking to the pastry board it always has to be sprinkled lightly and evenly with flour.

To prevent the dough from drying out during the resting phases, it has to be wrapped in a moist cloth.

Never press leftover dough together. Put the individual pieces flat on top of each other and roll out again.

Dough:

500 g	all-purpose flour	3⅓	cups
1 pkg	**oetker** instant dry yeast	1	pkg.
2 mL	salt	½	tsp.
5 drops	**oetker** lemon flavouring concentrate	5	drops
2	eggs	2	
2	egg yolks	2	
50 g	melted butter or margarine	¼	cup
approx 150 mL	lukewarm milk	⅔	cup

Butter "Brick"

200 g	butter or margarine, softened	1	cup
50 g	all-purpose flour	⅓	cup

1. COMBINE flour and yeast in large bowl.

2. MAKE a well in centre. PUT salt, **oetker** flavouring concentrate, eggs, egg yolks, butter and milk into well.

3. KNEAD dough with dough hooks or by hand, until smooth, elastic and blistered in appearance, about 5 minutes. COVER with a cloth and let rise in warm place until doubled in size, about 1 hour. ROLL out into a rectangle (about 30×25 cm / 12″×10″).
cm.

4. For butter "brick" combine soft butter and flour, until smooth. Shape into a "brick" (20×10 cm / 8″×4″). Chill until firm. Place brick in middle of dough rectangle.

5. Brush sides of dough lightly with water. Fold dough over butter "brick" and press sides together. The butter has to be completely wrapped in the dough. Carefully roll out to a rectangle (about 30×40 cm / 12″×16″).

6. Fold narrow sides of dough into centre (like folding a towel) to create three layers. Chill for about 30 minutes. Repeat rolling and folding 2-3 times before continuing with chosen recipe.

Pizza Dough (Basic Recipe)

In its simplest form the pizza was most likely known long before the discovery of America. Today it is not only a favourite in Italy but also in many countries and its many variations and flavours – delicate, strong, hot and spicy or even sweet – are popular everywhere.

The classical shape – round and plate size – is the most popular. Mini pizzas are ideal for parties as hors d'oeuvres. The simplest shape, rectangular, baking sheet size, is easy for cutting and serving.

The dough can be prepared in large quantities and kept, following proper storage instructions, for a long period of time.

Pizza dough, well wrapped, may be stored in the refrigerator for a period of two days.

Frozen (preferably in portion size) it may be stored for up to five months. The dough should be rolled out into circular shapes, pre-frozen, and wrapped airtight, be stored in the freezer. When needed, place the frozen dough onto a greased baking sheet. Let thaw, distribute filling evenly over dough, and bake as directed in recipe.

Dough:

300	g	all-purpose flour	2	cups
1	pkg	**oetker** instant dry yeast	1	pkg.
5	mL	salt	1	tsp.
175	mL	lukewarm water	¾	cup
30	mL	olive oil	2	tbsp.

1. Sift flour.

2. COMBINE flour and **oetker** instant dry yeast in large bowl. Make a well in centre.

3. PUT salt, water and olive oil into well.

4. KNEAD dough with dough hooks or by hand, until smooth, elastic, blistery and no longer sticky, about 5 minutes.

5. KNEAD lightly by hand until smooth. Shape into a ball.

6. LET rise, covered, in warm place, about 30 minutes.

Brioche Dough (Basic Recipe)

Freshly baked brioche is the "queen" of the yeast doughs. It is very delicate and has an incredibly delicious taste due to its high butter and egg content.

Brioche can be baked in a variety of different shapes – the most well known among them are individual brioche portions.

Use only very fresh butter, preferably unsalted, for preparing the brioche dough.

In order to achieve the delicate porous texture, the dough should be prepared a day ahead and allowed to rise in the refrigerator.

Brioche dough can be frozen without loss in quality of taste. Because of the high butter content, up to a ratio of 1:1 compared to flour, it should not be stored for more than one month.

Before use, thaw slowly in the refrigerator (about 24 hours).

Since the dough is relatively heavy, it requires a longer rising time than other basic yeast recipes. Under no circumstances should this time period be shortened by exposing the dough to a higher temperature.

Dough:

475	g	all-purpose flour	3¼ cups
1	pkg	**oetker** instant dry yeast	1 pkg.
25	g	sugar	2 tbsp.
1	pkg	**oetker** vanilla sugar	1 pkg.
	pinch	salt	pinch
½	btl	**oetker** lemon flavouring concentrate	½ btl.
3		eggs	3
150	mL	lukewarm milk	⅔ cup
125	g	butter or margarine, softened	½ cup

1. SIFT Flour.

2. COMBINE flour and **oetker** instant dry yeast in large bowl. Make a well in centre.

3. PUT sugar, **oetker** vanilla sugar, salt, **oetker** flavouring concentrate and eggs into well. Work flour into centre ingredients, gradually adding milk.

4. KNEAD dough with dough hooks or by hand, until smooth, blistery, and no longer sticky, about 5 minutes.

5. ADD soft butter and continue kneading dough, until it is elastic and shiny in appearance. It should have a very elastic consistency without tearing.

6. CHILL covered dough for about 2 hours. Knead dough again; cover and chill overnight. Continue with desired recipe the following day.

Plum Streusel Cake

Dough:

300 g	all-purpose flour	2	cups
1 pkg	**oetker** instant dry yeast	1	pkg.
2 mL	salt	½	tsp.
25 g	sugar	2	tbsp.
1 pkg	**oetker** vanilla sugar	1	pkg.
½ btl	**oetker** lemon flavouring concentrate	½	btl.
2	egg yolks	2	
50 g	melted butter or margarine	¼	cup
approx 125 mL	lukewarm milk	½	cup
25 g	melted butter or margarine	2	tbsp.

Filling:

100 g	ground hazelnuts or walnuts	1	cup
50 g	dry breadcrumbs	½	cup
75 g	sugar	⅓	cup
1 pkg	**oetker** vanilla sugar	1	pkg.
5 mL	ground cinnamon	1	tsp.
5 drops	**oetker** rum flavouring concentrate	5	drops
50 g	raisins	½	cup
50 mL	hot milk	¼	cup
15 mL	liquid honey	1	tbsp.

Crumb Topping:

80 g	all-purpose flour	½	cup
25 g	sugar	2	tbsp.
25 g	ground almonds	¼	cup
50 g	butter or margarine, softened	¼	cup
100 g	plum jam	½	cup

Method:

PREHEAT oven to 180°C (350°F). Grease a 26 cm (10½") springform pan. Sprinkle lightly with dry bread crumbs.

PREPARE dough using method in basic recipe #351.

ROLL out ½ of dough on floured surface to a 30 cm (12") circle. Place in bottom of springform pan and press dough 3 cm (1½") up side of pan.

BRUSH dough lightly with melted butter.

Filling:

COMBINE all ingredients. Mix well.

SPREAD ½ of filling on dough in pan.

ROLL out ½ of remaining dough to a 26 cm (10½") circle and place over filling.

BRUSH lightly with melted butter.

SPREAD with remaining filling.

ROLL out remaining dough as above and place over filling.

Crumb Topping:

COMBINE flour, sugar and ground almonds.

CUT in butter, working it with fork until crumbly.

BRUSH top dough layer with plum jam.

SPRINKLE crumbs evenly over jam.

LET RISE, covered, in warm place, about 30 minutes.

PIERCE several times with a fork.

BAKE on lower oven rack at 180°C (350°F) for 50-60 minutes.

Grandma's Coffee Cake

Dough:

500 g	all-purpose flour	3⅓	cups
1 pkg	**oetker** instant dry yeast	1	pkg.
5 mL	salt	1	tsp.
75 g	sugar	⅓	cup
1 pkg	**oetker** vanilla sugar	1	pkg.
½ btl	**oetker** lemon flavouring concentrate	½	btl.
2	eggs	2	
80 g	melted butter or margarine	⅓	cup
250 mL	lukewarm milk	1	cup

Filling:

125 mL	plum jam	½	cup
1	egg, slightly beaten	1	

Method:
PREHEAT oven to 180°C (350°F). Grease and flour a baking sheet.
PREPARE dough, using method in basic recipe #351.
DIVIDE ⅔ of dough into 8 parts. Roll out a little.
BRUSH with plum jam.
SHAPE into 8 rounds.
PLACE closely together on prepared baking sheet, forming a circle.
SHAPE remaining dough into 16 small rounds.
PLACE 8 inside and 8 outside of circle, touching larger rounds (see picture).
LET RISE, covered, in warm place, about 30 minutes.
BRUSH lightly with beaten egg.
BAKE on middle oven rack at 180°C (350°F) for 30-40 minutes.

Apple Meringue Squares

Dough:

250 g	all-purpose flour	1⅔	cups
½ pkg	**oetker** instant dry yeast	½	pkg.
pinch	salt	pinch	
25 g	sugar	2	tbsp.
1 pkg	**oetker** vanilla sugar	1	pkg.
3 drops	**oetker** lemon flavouring concentrate	3	drops
2	egg yolks	2	
40 g	melted butter or margarine	3	tbsp.
approx 125 mL	lukewarm milk	½	cup

Topping:

	melted butter or margarine		
100 g	sugar	½	cup
15 mL	ground cinnamon	1	tbsp.
800 g	apples	1¾	lb.
	juice of 1 lemon		

Decoration:

4	egg whites	4	
80 g	sugar	⅓	cup
30 g	icing sugar, sifted	¼	cup

Method:
PREHEAT oven to 180°C (350°F). Grease and flour a baking sheet.
PREPARE dough using method in basic recipe #351.
SPREAD or roll dough evenly on prepared baking sheet.

Topping:
BRUSH dough lightly with melted butter.
SPRINKLE evenly with sugar and cinnamon.
PEEL and core apples. CUT into thin slices.
SPRINKLE with lemon juice.
COVER dough evenly with apple slices.
LET RISE, covered, in warm place, about 30 minutes.
BAKE on middle oven rack at 180°C (350°F) for 25-30 minutes.
DECORATE immediately.

Decoration:
BEAT egg whites to soft peaks. Gradually add sugar, beating to stiff peaks.
FILL into pastry bag with star tip. Pipe in lattice design onto baked cake.
SPRINKLE with icing sugar.
BAKE at 180°C (350°F) for 10 more minutes.
CUT into diamonds or squares.

Fruit Bundt Cake

Dough:
Basic recipe #351

1	egg white, slightly beaten	1

Filling:

200 g	ground hazelnuts	2 cups
60 mL	rum	¼ cup
50 g	sugar	¼ cup
1 pkg	**oetker** vanilla sugar	1 pkg.
40 g	chopped dried figs	1½ oz.
40 g	chopped dates	1½ oz.
40 g	chopped candied lemon peel	1½ oz.
40 g	chopped candied orange peel	1½ oz.
40 g	chopped dried apricots	1½ oz.
40 g	chopped prunes	1½ oz.
50 mL	strained apricot jam	¼ cup

Glaze:

200 g	icing sugar, sifted	1½ cups
15 mL	lemon juice	1 tbsp.
15-30 mL	hot water	1-2 tbsp.

Decoration:

50 g	chopped candied cherries	¼ cup
20 g	chopped pistachio nuts	¼ cup

Method:
PREHEAT oven to 180°C (350°F). Grease and flour a bundt or tube pan.
PREPARE dough using method in basic recipe #351.
ROLL out dough on floured surface to .5 cm (¼") thick rectangle.
BRUSH dough with egg white.
Filling:
COMBINE all ingredients, except jam. Mix well.
SPREAD evenly over dough.
ROLL up dough starting at long side.
PLACE in prepared bundt or tube pan.
LET RISE, covered, in warm place, about 30 minutes.
Pierce with a fork several times.
BAKE on lower oven rack at 180°C (350°F) for 50-60 minutes.
BRUSH jam over hot cake.
Glaze:
COMBINE icing sugar, lemon juice and enough water to make a smooth glaze consistency.
SPREAD glaze over top and sides of cake.
SPRINKLE with candied cherries and pistachios.

Chocolate Nut Bars

Dough:
Basic recipe #352

Filling:

200 g	ground walnuts or almonds	2 cups
100 g	sugar	½ cup
1 pkg	**oetker** vanilla sugar	1 pkg.
75 mL	milk	⅓ cup
5 drops	**oetker** rum flavouring concentrate	5 drops
50 g	melted butter or margarine	¼ cup
50 g	semi-sweet chocolate, melted	2 sq.
5 mL	ground cinnamon	1 tsp.

Decoration:

50 g	semi-sweet chocolate, melted	2 sq.

Method:
PREHEAT oven to 180°C (350°F). Grease a 3.5 L (9" × 13") cake pan.
PREPARE dough, using method in basic recipe #352.
PRESS into prepared pan.
Filling:
COMBINE all ingredients. Mix well.
SPREAD evenly over dough.
BAKE on middle oven rack at 180°C (350°F) for 25-30 minutes.
COOL completely.
DECORATE attractively with melted chocolate.
CUT into bars.

Almond Bundt Cake

Dough:

150 g	whole blanched almonds	1	cup
500 g	all-purpose flour	3⅓	cups
1 pkg	**oetker** instant dry yeast	1	pkg.
100 g	sugar	½	cup
1 pkg	**oetker** vanilla sugar	1	pkg.
2 mL	salt	½	tsp.
1	egg	1	
3	egg yolks	3	
125 g	melted butter or margarine	½	cup
125 mL	lukewarm milk	½	cup
100 g	raisins	1	cup

Decoration:

icing sugar, sifted

Dough:

PREHEAT oven to 180°C (350°F). Grease and flour a bundt pan. Place almonds evenly into bundt pan.
PREPARE dough with listed ingredients except raisins and method in basic recipe #351.
LET RISE, covered, in warm place, about 30 minutes.
KNEAD raisins into dough.
TURN dough into prepared bundt pan.
LET RISE, covered, in warm place, about 30 minutes.
BAKE on lower oven rack at 180°C (350°F) for 50-60 minutes.
COOL.
SPRINKLE with icing sugar before serving.

Hazelnut Wreath

Dough:

450 g	all-purpose flour	3	cups
1 pkg	**oetker** instant dry yeast	1	pkg.
50 g	sugar	¼	cup
1 pkg	**oetker** vanilla sugar	1	pkg.
2 mL	salt	½	tsp.
5 drops	**oetker** lemon flavouring concentrate	5	drops
1	egg	1	
50 g	butter or margarine, softened	¼	cup
250 mL	lukewarm milk	1	cup
1	egg, slightly beaten	1	

Filling:

125 mL	milk	½	cup
100 g	sugar	½	cup
1 pkg	**oetker** vanilla sugar	1	pkg.
½ btl	**oetker** rum flavouring concentrate	½	btl.
200 g	ground hazelnuts	2	cups

Decoration:

60-75 mL	strained apricot jam	4-5	tbsp.
30 g	ground or finely chopped hazelnuts	⅓	cup

Method:

PREHEAT oven to 180°C (350°F). Grease and flour a 24 cm (9½") tube pan.
PREPARE dough with listed ingredients and method in basic recipe #351.
ROLL out dough on floured surface to a .5 cm (¼") thick rectangle.
BRUSH dough with beaten egg.
Filling:
BRING milk, sugar, vanilla sugar and flavouring to a boil.
ADD hazelnuts, mix well and let cool.
SPREAD evenly over dough.
ROLL up dough starting from long side.
PLACE into prepared tube pan.
LET RISE, covered, in warm place, about 30 minutes.
BRUSH with beaten egg. Pierce with a fork several times.
BAKE on lower oven rack at 180°C (350°F) for 45-50 minutes.
SPREAD jam over hot cake.
SPRINKLE with hazelnuts.

Apple Strudel

Dough:

300 g	all-purpose flour	2	cups
½ pkg	**oetker** instant dry yeast	½	pkg.
25 g	sugar	2	tbsp.
1 pkg	**oetker** vanilla sugar	1	pkg.
pinch	salt		pinch
3 drops	**oetker** lemon flavouring concentrate	3	drops
1	egg	1	
30 g	melted butter or margarine	2	tsp.
approx 125 mL	lukewarm milk	½	cup
1	egg, slightly beaten	1	

Filling:

750 g	apples	1½	lbs.
15 mL	rum	1	tbsp.
	juice of 1 lemon		
100 g	sugar	½	cup
15 mL	ground cinnamon	1	tbsp.
50 g	raisins	½	cup
30 g	icing sugar, sifted	¼	cup

Method:
PREHEAT oven to 180°C (350°F). Grease and flour a baking sheet.
PREPARE dough with listed ingredients, using method in basic recipe #351.
ROLL out dough on floured surface to a .5 cm (¼″) thick rectangle.
BRUSH dough with beaten egg.
Filling:
PEEL and core apples; cut into thin slices.
SPRINKLE with rum and lemon juice.
SPREAD apples, sugar, cinnamon and raisins evenly over dough.
ROLL up dough tightly, starting at long side.
PLACE on prepared baking sheet.
LET RISE, covered, in warm place, about 30 minutes.
BRUSH with beaten egg. Pierce with a fork several times.
BAKE on middle oven rack at 180°C (350°F) for 30-35 minutes.
COOL.
SPRINKLE with icing sugar before serving.

Wasps' Nests

Dough:
Basic recipe #351
Filling:

approx 50 g	melted butter or margarine	¼	cup
100 g	coarse or regular granulated sugar	½	cup
50 g	sliced almonds	½	cup
100 g	raisins	1	cup

Glaze:

100 g	sugar	½	cup
125 mL	water	½	cup

Method:
PREHEAT oven to 180°C (350°F). Grease a 3.5 L (9″×13″) cake pan.
PREPARE dough using ingredients and method in basic recipe #351.
ROLL out dough on floured surface to a 35 cm × 25 cm (14″×10″) rectangle, 1 cm (½″) thick.
BRUSH with melted butter.
SPRINKLE with sugar, almonds and raisins.
ROLL up dough starting at long side.
CUT into twelve slices about 3 cm (1″) thick.
PLACE into prepared baking pan, not too closely together.
BRUSH with melted butter.
LET RISE, covered, 45-60 minutes.
BAKE on lower oven rack at 180°C (350°F) for 20-25 minutes.
Glaze:
COMBINE sugar and water in small saucepan.
SIMMER about 15 minutes, or until thickened.
BRUSH evenly over cake.

Brioche Muffins

Dough:
Brioche basic recipe #355

1	egg yolk	1
5 mL	milk	1 tsp.

Method:
PREHEAT oven to 220°C (425°F). Grease 15 muffin cups.
PREPARE dough using ingredients and method in basic recipe #355.
LET RISE, covered, in warm place, about 1 hour.
TURN out onto a floured surface and shape into a roll.
CUT into 15 even slices.
CUT off ⅓ of each slice. Shape pieces into 15 large and 15 small balls.
PLACE large dough balls into prepared muffin pans, make a well in centre of each.
COMBINE egg yolk and milk thoroughly. Brush each well with egg mixture.
PLACE a small dough ball in each well.
LET RISE, covered, until doubled in size, about 25 minutes.
BRUSH with egg mixture.
BAKE on middle oven rack at 220°C (425°F) for 20-30 minutes.
REMOVE immediately from pan. Let cool.

Almond Torte

Dough:
Basic recipe #352
Filling:

3	egg whites	3
60 g	coarse or regular granulated sugar	⅓ cup
100 g	icing sugar, sifted	¾ cup
1 pkg	**oetker** vanilla sugar	1 pkg.
200 g	chopped almonds	2 cups
5 mL	ground cinnamon	1 tsp.

Decoration:

30 g	icing sugar, sifted	¼ cup
	sliced almonds	

Method:
PREHEAT oven to 180°C (350°F). Grease a 24 cm (9½″) springform pan. Remove rim.
PREPARE dough using ingredients and method in basic recipe #352.
PRESS or roll ½ of dough onto bottom of prepared pan. Replace rim.
SHAPE remaining dough into a long roll, press around inside rim of pan forming 3 cm (1¼″) high sides. Press seams to seal well.
Filling:
BEAT egg whites to soft peaks. Gradually add granulated sugar, beating to stiff peaks.
COMBINE icing sugar, vanilla sugar, almonds and cinnamon.
FOLD into egg whites gently.
SPREAD evenly over dough.
BAKE on lower oven rack at 180°C (350°F) for 35-40 minutes.
COOL.
SPRINKLE attractively with icing sugar and almonds.

DEEP FRIED

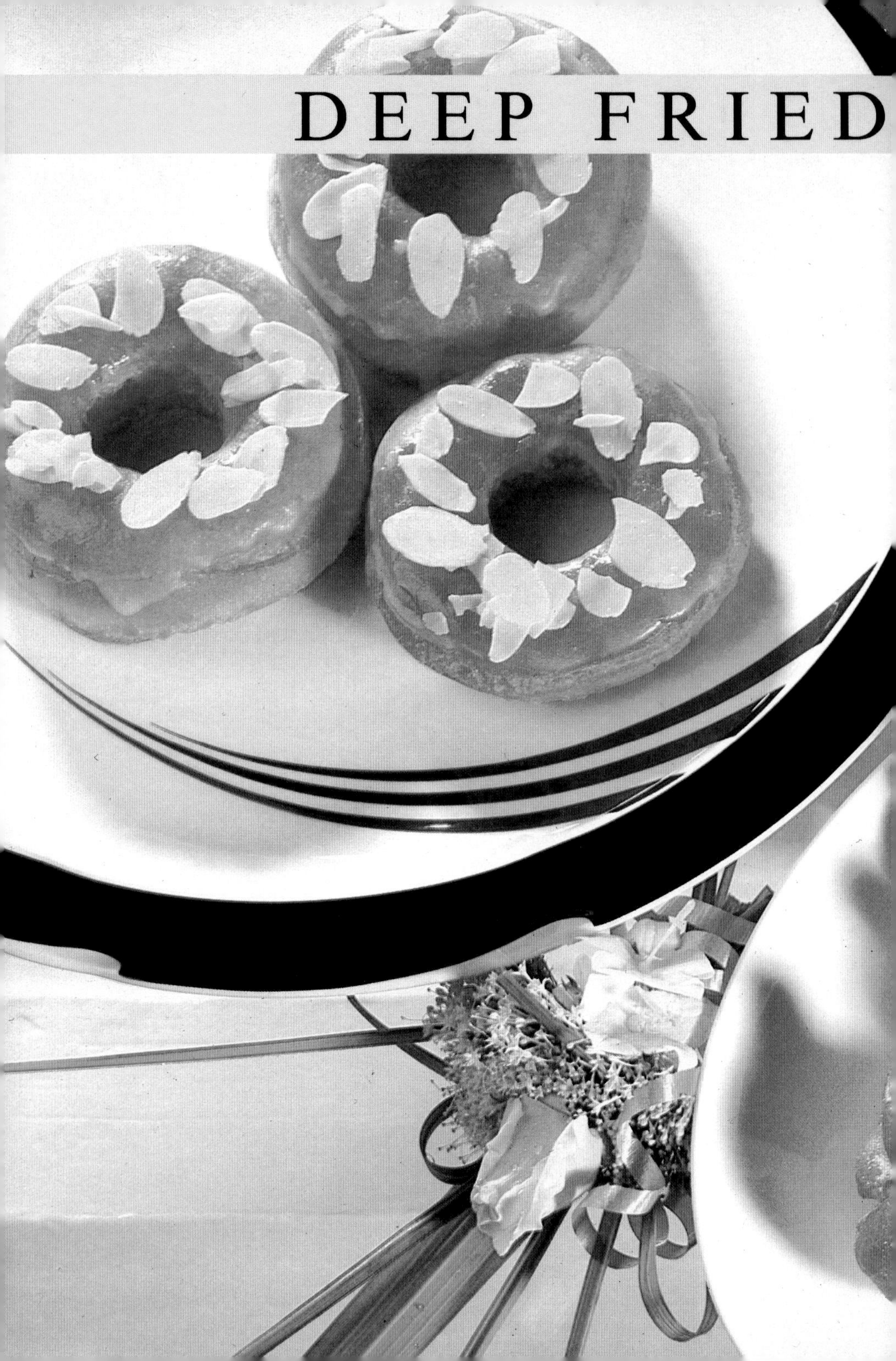

DELICACIES

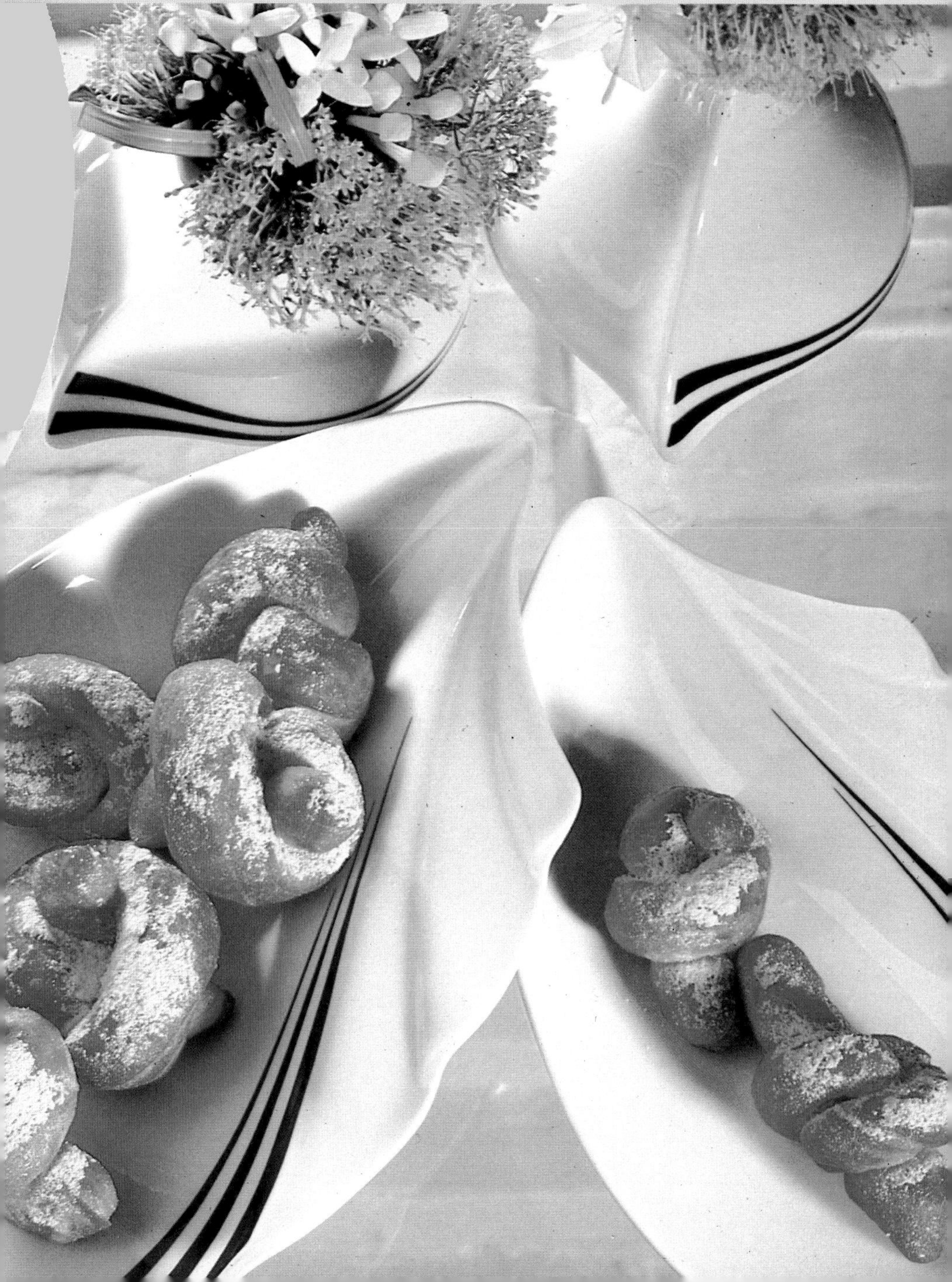

Almond Doughnuts

Dough:

500 g	all-purpose flour	3⅓ cups	
1 pkg	**oetker** instant dry yeast	1 pkg.	
5 mL	salt	1 tsp.	
50 g	sugar	¼ cup	
1 pkg	**oetker** vanilla sugar	1 pkg.	
½ btl	**oetker** lemon flavouring concentrate	½ btl.	
45 mL	rum	3 tbsp.	
2	eggs	2	
1	egg yolk	1	
50 g	melted butter or margarine	¼ cup	
125 mL	lukewarm milk	½ cup	

Filling:

100 g	marzipan	3 oz.
50 g	sugar	¼ cup
1 pkg	**oetker** vanilla sugar	1 pkg.
50 g	chopped almonds	½ cup
1	egg white, unbeaten	1

For deep frying:

oil or shortening

Decoration:

150 g	icing sugar, sifted	1 cup
30-45 mL	lemon juice	2-3 tbsp.
50 mL	toasted sliced almonds	¼ cup

Method:
PREPARE dough using method in basic recipe #351.
ROLL out dough on floured surface to about .5 cm (¼″) thickness.
CUT into 8 cm (3″) rounds with floured cutter.
Filling:
COMBINE all ingredients. Mix well.
PUT filling into decorating bag with small round tube.
PIPE filling in a circle on half the rounds leaving 1 cm (½″) edge. Moisten edges.
PLACE remaining rounds over filling. Press edges together to seal completely.
CUT small hole about 2 cm (¾″) in centre of rounds to form rings.
LET RISE about 20 minutes.
HEAT fat to 190°C (375°F). Keep at an even temperature.
FRY rounds, a few at a time, until golden brown on both sides.
REMOVE from fat. Drain well on paper towelling.
BLEND sifted icing sugar and enough lemon juice to make a smooth glaze consistency.
SPREAD over rings.
SPRINKLE with sliced almonds.

Sugar Twists

Dough:

450 g	all-purpose flour	3 cups	
1 pkg	**oetker** active dry yeast	1 pkg.	
75 g	sugar	⅓ cup	
1 pkg	**oetker** vanilla sugar	1 pkg.	
pinch	salt	pinch	
½ btl	**oetker** lemon flavouring concentrate	½ btl.	
4	egg yolks	4	
75 g	melted butter or margarine	⅓ cup	
250 mL	lukewarm milk	1 cup	

For deep frying:

oil or shortening

Decoration:

30 g	icing sugar, sifted	¼ cup
1 mL	ground cinnamon	¼ tsp.

Method:
COMBINE flour and yeast in large mixing bowl. Make a well in centre.
PUT sugar, vanilla sugar, salt, lemon flavouring, egg yolks and melted butter in well.
WORK flour into centre ingredients, gradually adding milk.
KNEAD dough with dough hooks or by hand until blistered and shiny in appearance, and no longer sticky, about 5 minutes.
LET RISE, covered, in warm place until doubled in size, about 1 hour.
DIVIDE dough into 25 pieces.
SHAPE each into 15 cm (6″) rolls.
FORM each roll loosely into a knot.
LET RISE about 20 minutes.
HEAT fat to 190°C (375°F). Keep at an even temperature.
FRY knots, a few at a time, until golden brown on both sides.
REMOVE from fat. Drain well on paper towelling.
SPRINKLE with mixture of icing sugar and cinnamon.

Vanilla Cream Filled Doughnuts

Dough:

500 g	all-purpose flour	3⅓	cup
1 pkg	**oetker** instant dry yeast	1	pkg.
5 mL	salt	1	tsp.
50 g	sugar	¼	cup
1 pkg	**oetker** vanilla sugar	1	pkg.
½ btl	**oetker** lemon flavouring concentrate	½	btl.
½ btl	**oetker** rum flavouring concentrate	½	btl.
2	eggs	2	
50 g	melted butter or margarine	¼	cup
50 mL approx	whipping cream	¼	cup
125 mL	lukewarm milk	½	cup

For deep frying:

oil or shortening

Filling:

1 pkg	**oetker** vanilla pudding powder	1	pkg.
30 mL	sugar	2	tbsp.
500 mL	milk	2	cups
15-30 mL	rum	1-2	tbsp.

Decoration:

30 g	icing sugar, sifted	¼	cup

Method:

PREPARE dough using method in basic recipe #351.
LET dough rise 1 hour.
ROLL out dough on floured surface to about 1 cm (½") thickness.
CUT out into 8 cm (3") rounds with floured cutter.
LET RISE, covered, in warm place, until doubled in size, about 30 minutes.
HEAT fat to 190°C (375°F), Keep at an even temperature.
FRY doughnuts, a few at a time, 1 minute on each side, or until golden brown.
TURN doughnuts, fry, uncovered, until other side is golden brown.
REMOVE from fat. Drain on paper towelling.
Filling:
PREPARE according to directions on package.
STIR rum into mixture.
LET cool, stirring frequently.
PUT filling in decorating bag with small round tube.
SQUIRT small amount carefully into doughnuts, inserting decorating tube carefully at white band in centre on sides of doughnuts.
SPRINKLE with icing sugar.

Twisted Doughnut Squares

Dough:

500 g	all-purpose flour	3⅓	cups
1 pkg	**oetker** instant dry yeast	1	pkg.
pinch	salt		pinch
100 g	sugar	½	cup
1 pkg	**oetker** vanilla sugar	1	pkg.
3	eggs	3	
5 mL	ground cinnamon	1	tsp.
pinch	ground cloves		pinch
50 g	melted butter or margarine	¼	cup
250 mL	lukewarm milk	1	cup
50 g	raisins	½	cup

For deep frying:

oil or shortening

Decoration:

30 g	icing sugar, sifted	¼	cup
1 mL	ground cinnamon	¼	tsp.

Method:

PREPARE dough using method in basic recipe #351.
KNEAD raisins into dough.
ROLL out dough on floured surface to approx. .5 cm (¼") thickness.
CUT into squares 5 cm×5 cm (2"×2").
LEAVING outside borders intact, cut each square into 4 strips of 1 cm (½) width.
HEAT fat to 190°C (375°F). Keep at an even temperature.
PLACE alternate strips of each square, a few at a time, on handle of wooden spoon.
FRY until golden brown on both sides.
REMOVE from fat. Drain well on paper towelling.
SPRINKLE with mixture of icing sugar and cinnamon.

Pretzels

Dough:

500 g	all-purpose flour	3⅓	cups
1 pkg	**oetker** instant dry yeast	1	pkg.
pinch	salt		pinch
50 g	sugar	¼	cup
1 pkg	**oetker** vanilla sugar	1	pkg.
pinch	ground allspice		pinch
pinch	ground ginger		pinch
45 mL	rum	3	tbsp.
½ btl	**oetker** lemon flavouring concentrate	½	btl.
1	egg	1	
75 g	melted butter or margarine	⅓	cup
approx 175 mL	lukewarm milk	¾	cup

For deep frying:

oil or shortening

Decoration:

30 g	icing sugar, sifted	¼	cup

Method:
PREPARE dough using method in basic recipe #351.
DIVIDE dough into 20 pieces.
ROLL into long ropes and twist into pretzel shape.
LET RISE, covered, in warm place, about 20 minutes.
HEAT fat to 190°C (375°F). Keep at an even temperature.
FRY pretzels, a few at a time, until golden brown on both sides.
REMOVE from fat. Drain well on paper towelling.
SPRINKLE with icing sugar.

Saffron Braids

Dough:

150 mL	lukewarm milk	⅔	cup
5	saffron threads	5	
500 g	all-purpose flour	3⅓	cups
1 pkg	**oetker** instant dry yeast	1	pkg.
pinch	salt		pinch
50 g	sugar	¼	cup
1 pkg	**oetker** vanilla sugar	1	pkg.
½ btl	**oetker** lemon flavouring concentrate	½	btl.
45 mL	rum	3	tbsp.
2	eggs	2	
100 g	melted butter or margarine	½	cup

For deep frying:

oil or shortening

Decoration:

100 g	icing sugar, sifted	⅔	cup
2 pkg	**oetker** natural vanilla sugar	2	pkg.

Method:
DISSOLVE saffron in milk.
PREPARE dough using method in basic recipe #351.
DIVIDE dough into 15 pieces.
ROLL into ropes and shape into braids.
LET RISE, covered, in warm place, about 20 minutes.
HEAT fat to 190°C (375°F). Keep at an even temperature.
FRY, a few pieces at a time, until golden brown on both sides.
REMOVE from fat. Drain well on paper towelling.
SPRINKLE with mixture of icing sugar and natural vanilla sugar.

Nut Delights in Caramel Sauce

Dough:

450 g	all-purpose flour	3	cups
1 pkg	**oetker** active dry yeast	1	pkg.
75 g	sugar	⅓	cup
1 pkg	**oetker** vanilla sugar	1	pkg.
pinch	salt		pinch
½ btl	**oetker** lemon flavouring concentrate	½	btl.
4	egg yolks	4	
75 g	melted butter or margarine	⅓	cup
250 mL	lukewarm milk	1	cup

Filling:

150 g	ground walnuts or hazelnuts	1½	cups
100 g	sugar	½	cup
1 pkg	**oetker** natural vanilla sugar	1	pkg.
5 mL	ground cinnamon	1	tsp.
5 drops	**oetker** rum flavouring concentrate	5	drops
15 mL	liquid honey	1	tbsp.
75 mL	hot milk	⅓	cup
	melted butter or margarine		

Caramel Sauce:

100 g	sugar	½	cup
500 mL	milk	2	cups
2 pkg	**oetker** vanilla sauce	2	pkg.

Decoration:

15 g	icing sugar, sifted	2	tbsp.

Method:
PREHEAT oven to 180°C (350°F). Grease square cake pan.
COMBINE flour and yeast in large bowl. Make a well in centre. PUT sugar, vanilla sugar, salt, lemon flavouring, egg yolks and melted butter in well.
WORK flour into centre ingredients, gradually add milk.
KNEAD dough with dough hooks or by hand until blistered and shiny in appearance and no longer sticky, about 5 minutes. PLACE in greased bowl. LET RISE, covered in warm place until doubled in size, about 1 hour.
SHAPE dough into a 3 cm (1¼″) diameter roll.
DIVIDE into pieces 5 cm (2″) long.
MAKE a well in centre of each. Fill with 5 mL (1 tsp.) nut filling.
PRESS down ends to form a tight seal.
BRUSH with melted butter. PLACE in prepared pan.
LET RISE in warm place about 15 minutes.
BAKE on lower oven rack at 180°C (350°F) for 40-45 minutes.
Filling:
COMBINE all ingredients. Mix well.
Caramel Sauce:
MELT sugar in saucepan until caramel coloured.
ADD milk carefully; bring to a boil.
COOK until all sugar is dissolved, stirring constantly.
REMOVE milk mixture from stove.
ADD vanilla sauce powder to mixture, stirring constantly for 1 minute, until powder is dissolved. Return to heat, bring just to a boil, then remove from heat.
SPRINKLE nut delights with icing sugar. Serve with caramel sauce.

Pear Nests

Dough:

450 g	all-purpose flour	3	cups
1 pkg	**oetker** active dry yeast	1	pkg.
75 g	sugar	⅓	cup
1 pkg	**oetker** vanilla sugar	1	pkg.
pinch	salt		pinch
½ btl	**oetker** lemon flavouring concentrate	½	btl.
4	egg yolks	4	
75 g	melted butter or margarine	⅓	cup
250 mL	lukewarm milk	1	cup

Butter "Brick":

150 g	butter, softened	¾	cup
40 g	sifted all-purpose flour	¼	cup
1	egg, slightly beaten	1	
1 kg	steamed or canned pear halves	2	lbs.

Vanilla Sauce:

1 pkg	**oetker** vanilla pudding powder	1	pkg.
50 g	sugar	¼	cup
875 mL	milk	3½	cups

Method:
PREHEAT oven to 180°C (350°F). Grease and flour a baking sheet.
COMBINE flour and yeast in large bowl. Make a well in centre. PUT sugar, vanilla sugar, salt, lemon flavouring, egg yolks and melted butter in well.
WORK flour into centre ingredients, gradually add milk.
KNEAD dough with dough hooks or by hand until blistered and shiny in appearance and no longer sticky, about 5 minutes. LET RISE, covered, in warm place until doubled in size, about 1 hour.
ROLL out dough on floured surface to about .5 cm (¼″) thickness.
CONTINUE as per point 4 in basic recipe #353.
ROLL out dough on floured surface to about .5 cm (¼″) thickness. BRUSH with beaten egg.
PLACE pear halves onto dough, leaving 3 cm (1¼″) spaces between each half. CUT out leaves from leftover dough. Brush with beaten egg. Press tightly onto pear nests.
PLACE dough onto prepared baking sheet.
LET RISE, covered, about 20 minutes.
BAKE on middle oven rack at 180°C (350°F) for 15-20 minutes.
PREPARE vanilla sauce according to package directions, using above ingredients. Serve with pear nests.

Russian Baba

Dough:

350 g	all-purpose flour	2⅓	cups
1 pkg	**oetker** instant dry yeast	1	pkg.
50 g	sugar	¼	cup
1 pkg	**oetker** vanilla sugar	1	pkg.
2 mL	salt	½	tsp.
6 drops	**oetker** lemon flavouring concentrate	6	drops
2	eggs	2	
2	egg yolks	2	
50 mL	whipping cream	¼	cup
50 g	melted butter or margarine	¼	cup
125 mL	lukewarm milk	½	cup

Syrup:

250 mL	water	1	cup
	juice of 1 orange		
150 g	sugar	¾	cup
75 mL	rum	⅓	cup

Chocolate Sauce:

125 mL	milk	½	cup
100 g	semi-sweet chocolate, chopped	4	sq.
250 g	fruit, as desired	8	oz.

Method:

PREHEAT oven to 180°C (350°F). Grease and flour small baba or ring pans.

COMBINE flour and yeast in large mixing bowl. Make a well in centre.

PUT sugar, vanilla sugar, salt, lemon flavouring, eggs, egg yolks, whipping cream and melted butter in well.

WORK flour into centre ingredients, gradually adding milk.

KNEAD dough with dough hooks or by hand until blistered and shiny in appearance and no longer sticky, about 5 minutes.

PLACE in greased bowl.

LET RISE, covered, in a warm place, about 30 minutes.

PLACE dough in prepared pans, filling half full.

LET RISE, covered, about 15 minutes.

BAKE on middle oven rack at 180°C (350°F) for 25-30 minutes.

REMOVE from pans immediately.

Syrup:

COMBINE water, orange juice and sugar in small saucepan. Bring to a boil.

STIR rum into mixture.

SPOON over hot cakes.

Chocolate Sauce:

Bring milk just to a boil.

ADD chocolate pieces, stirring constantly until smoothly melted.

Spoon fruit into centre of babas.

POUR sauce over babas.

Christmas Stollen

Dough:

500 g	all-purpose flour	3⅓	cups
1 pkg	**oetker** instant dry yeast	1	pkg.
50 g	sugar	¼	cup
1 pkg	**oetker** vanilla sugar	1	pkg.
pinch	salt		pinch
½ btl	**oetker** lemon flavouring concentrate	½	btl.
1 approx	egg	1	
75 mL	lukewarm milk	⅓	cup
175 g	butter or margarine, softened	¾	cup
100 g	all-purpose flour	⅔	cup
100 g	raisins	1	cup
50 g	currants	½	cup
40 g	sliced almonds	½	cup
60 g	chopped candied lemon peel	¼	cup
60 g	chopped candied orange peel	¼	cup
50 g	melted butter or margarine	¼	cup

Decoration:

100 g	icing sugar, sifted	⅔	cup

Method:
PREHEAT oven to 190°C (375°F). Grease and flour a baking sheet.
COMBINE ¾ of the flour and yeast in large bowl. Make a well in centre. PUT sugar, vanilla sugar, salt, lemon flavouring, egg and milk in well.
KNEAD dough with dough hooks or by hand until blistered and shiny in appearance, about 5 minutes.
ADD remaining flour. Knead well until no longer sticky.
PLACE in greased bowl.
LET RISE, covered, in warm place, about 15 minutes.
COMBINE soft butter and flour; stir well to a smooth paste. Add to dough; knead well.
LET RISE again, covered, about 15 minutes.
ADD raisins, currants, almonds, lemon and orange peel to dough. Knead well.
SHAPE dough into two loaves.
PLACE onto prepared baking sheet.
LET RISE, covered, in a warm place, about 20 minutes.
BAKE on middle oven rack at 190°C (375°F) for 20-25 minutes, or until golden.
BRUSH warm stollen with melted butter. Cool.
SPRINKLE with icing sugar before serving.

Santa Claus

Dough:

450 g	all-purpose flour	3	cups
1 pkg	**oetker** active dry yeast	1	pkg.
75 g	sugar	⅓	cup
1 pkg	**oetker** vanilla sugar	1	pkg.
pinch	salt		pinch
½ btl	**oetker** lemon flavouring concentrate	½	btl.
4	egg yolks	4	
75 g	melted butter or margarine	⅓	cup
250 mL	lukewarm milk	1	cup
1	egg, slightly beaten	1	

Glaze:

100 g	icing sugar, sifted	⅔	cup
30-45 mL	egg white, unbeaten	2-3	tbsp.

Method:
PREHEAT oven to 180°C (350°F). Grease and flour baking sheet.
COMBINE flour and yeast in large mixing bowl. Make a well in centre. PUT sugar, vanilla sugar, salt, lemon flavouring, egg yolks and melted butter in well.
WORK flour into centre ingredients, gradually add milk.
KNEAD dough with dough hooks or by hand until blistered and shiny in appearance, and no longer sticky, about 5 minutes.
PLACE in greased bowl.
LET RISE, covered, in warm place until doubled in size, about 1 hour.
KNEAD again.
SHAPE dough into a Santa Claus. (See photo for guide.)
PLACE onto prepared baking sheet.
LET RISE, covered, about 20 minutes.
BRUSH evenly with beaten egg.
BAKE on middle oven rack at 180°C (350°F) for 20-30 minutes. COOL.
Glaze:
COMBINE sifted icing sugar and enough egg white to make a thick smooth icing.
DECORATE as desired.

New Year's Pretzels

Dough:

	Basic recipe #353	
1	egg, slightly beaten	1
100 g	strained apricot jam	½ cup
	sugar sprinkles	

Method:
PREHEAT oven to 180°C (350°F). Grease and flour a baking sheet.
PREPARE dough, using method in basic recipe #353.
ROLL out dough on floured surface to about .5 cm (¼") thickness.
CUT into strips about 2 cm (¾") wide.
TWIST strips and form into pretzels. Press ends to seal.
PLACE onto prepared baking sheet.
LET RISE, covered, in warm place, about 20 minutes.
BRUSH evenly with beaten egg.
BAKE on middle oven rack at 180°C (350°F) for 15-20 minutes.
BRUSH jam evenly over warm pretzels.
DECORATE with sugar sprinkles.

Christmas Tree Surprise

Dough:

450 g	all-purpose flour	3 cups
1 pkg	**oetker** active dry yeast	1 pkg.
75 g	sugar	⅓ cup
1 pkg	**oetker** vanilla sugar	1 pkg.
pinch	salt	pinch
½ btl	**oetker** lemon flavouring concentrate	½ btl.
4	egg yolks	4
75 g	melted butter or margarine	⅓ cup
250 mL	lukewarm milk	1 cup

Filling:

100 g	ground hazelnuts	1 cup
30 g	sugar	2 tbsp.
1 pkg	**oetker** vanilla sugar	1 pkg.
2 mL	ground cinnamon	½ tsp.
30-45 mL	milk	2-3 tbsp.
1	egg, slightly beaten	1

Decoration:

30 mL	strained apricot jam	2 tbsp.
30 g	icing sugar, sifted	⅓ cup
	sugar sprinkles, optional	

Method:
PREHEAT oven to 180°C (350°F). Grease and flour a baking sheet.
COMBINE flour and yeast in large mixing bowl. Make a well in centre.
PUT sugar, vanilla sugar, salt, lemon flavouring, egg yolks and melted butter in well.
WORK flour into centre ingredients, gradually add milk.
KNEAD dough with dough hooks or by hand until blistered and shiny in appearance and no longer sticky, about 5 minutes. PLACE in greased bowl.
LET RISE, covered, in warm place until doubled in size, about 1 hour.
ROLL out dough on floured surface to about .5 cm (¼") thickness.
CUT out two Christmas trees, using photo as a guide.
Filling:
COMBINE all ingredients except egg. Mix well.
SPREAD evenly on one Christmas tree, leaving 1 cm (½") edge.
BRUSH edge with beaten egg.
PLACE second Christmas tree over filling. Press edges together to seal completely.
FORM shapes from dough scraps for tree ornaments.
PLACE tree and shapes onto prepared baking sheet.
LET RISE, covered, about 20 minutes.
BRUSH with beaten egg.
BAKE on middle oven rack at 180°C (350°F). Bake tree 20-25 minutes, shapes for 8-10 minutes.
BRUSH warm Christmas tree evenly with apricot jam.
COOL.
SPRINKLE with icing sugar.
DECORATE attractively with the baked shapes, and sugar sprinkles.

Lucky "Pig" Cookies

Dough:

500 g	all-purpose flour	3⅓	cups
1 pkg	**oetker** instant dry yeast	1	pkg.
75 g	sugar	⅓	cup
1 pkg	**oetker** vanilla sugar	1	pkg.
pinch	salt		pinch
1	egg	1	
60 g approx	melted butter or margarine	⅓	cup
60 g	lukewarm milk	⅓	cup
125 mL	grated rind of 1 lemon		

Filling:

200 g	ground hazelnuts	2	cups
150 g	sugar	¾	cup
1 pkg	**oetker** vanilla sugar	1	pkg.
1 mL	ground cinnamon	¼	tsp.
½ btl	**oetker** rum flavouring concentrate	½	btl.
1 approx	egg white	1	
50 mL	milk	¼	cup

Glaze:

1	egg yolk	1	
30 mL	milk	2	tbsp.

Method:
PREHEAT oven to 200°C (400°F). Grease and flour a baking sheet.
PREPARE dough, using method in basic recipe #351.
ROLL out dough on floured surface to about .5 cm (¼") thickness.
CUT out 20-30 rounds 8 cm (3") diameter and 10-15 rounds 4 cm (1½") in diameter.
SHAPE scraps of dough into pigs' ears.
Filling:
COMBINE all ingredients. Mix well.
PLACE filling on half of large rounds, leaving .5 cm (¼") edge.
BRUSH edges of these rounds with mixture of egg yolk and milk.
COVER with remaining large rounds. Press edges together to seal completely.
SHAPE small rounds into pigs' snouts. Make holes for nose. Place onto large rounds.
ATTACH ear shapes to rounds. Press firmly together.
USE raisins to form eyes.
BRUSH with mixture of egg yolk and milk.
PLACE onto prepared baking sheet.
LET RISE about 15 minutes.
BAKE on middle oven rack at 200°C (400°F) for 12-15 minutes.

Happy "Fish" Cookies

Dough:

450 g	all-purpose flour	3	cups
1 pkg	**oetker** active dry yeast	1	pkg.
75 g	sugar	⅓	cup
1 pkg	**oetker** vanilla sugar	1	pkg.
pinch	salt		pinch
½ btl	**oetker** lemon flavouring concentrate	½	btl.
4	egg yolks	4	
75 g	melted butter or margarine	⅓	cup
250 mL	lukewarm milk	1	cup

Glaze:

1	egg, slightly beaten	1	

Decoration:

100 g	icing sugar	⅔	cup
15-30 mL	lemon juice	1-2	tbsp.
	sugar sprinkles		

Method:
PREHEAT oven to 180°C (350°F). Grease and flour a baking sheet.
COMBINE flour and yeast in large bowl. Make a well in centre. PUT sugar, vanilla sugar, salt, lemon flavouring, egg yolks and melted butter in well.
WORK flour into centre ingredients, gradually add milk.
KNEAD dough with dough hooks or by hand until blistered and shiny in appearance and no longer sticky, about 5 minutes.
PLACE in greased bowl. LET RISE, covered, in warm place until doubled in size, about 1 hour.
ROLL out dough on floured surface to about .5 cm (¼") thickness.
CUT out rounds 8 cm (3") and 3 cm (1¼") in diameter. Pull large rounds into an oblong shape.
MAKE cuts into small rounds. Attach to large rounds with beaten egg, forming tail fins. To form fish scales, cut into dough of large rounds lightly.
PLACE on prepared baking sheet. LET RISE, covered, about 20 minutes. Brush with beaten egg. BAKE on middle oven rack at 180°C (350°F) for 15-20 minutes.
Glaze:
COMBINE sifted icing sugar and enough lemon juice to make a smooth thick icing.
DECORATE as desired.

Easter Bread

Dough:

500	g	all-purpose flour	3⅓	cups
1	pkg	**oetker** instant dry yeast	1	pkg.
75	g	sugar	⅓	cup
	pinch	salt		pinch
2	mL	ground nutmeg	½	tsp.
2	mL	ground allspice	½	tsp.
2		eggs	2	
100	g	melted butter or margarine	½	cup
approx				
250	mL	lukewarm milk	1	cup
50	g	raisins	½	cup

Glaze:

1		egg, slightly beaten	1

Method:
PREHEAT oven to 180°C (350°F). Grease a 25 cm (10″) springform pan.
PREPARE dough using method in basic recipe #351.
KNEAD raisins into dough.
DIVIDE into 4 pieces. Shape into 4 rounds.
PLACE into prepared springform pan.
LET RISE, covered, in warm place, about 20 minutes.
BRUSH with beaten egg.
BAKE on middle oven rack at 180°C (350°F) for 25-30 minutes.

Easter "Lamb" Bread

Dough:

Basic recipe #351

1		egg, slightly beaten	1	
15	g	icing sugar, sifted	2	tbsp.

Method:
PREHEAT oven to 180°C (350°F). Grease and flour a baking sheet.
PREPARE dough using method in basic recipe #351.
DIVIDE into 2 halves.
USE one half to shape body, head and legs of lamb on prepared baking sheet. (See photo for a guide).
BRUSH with beaten egg. Press firmly together.
SHAPE second half of dough into thin rolls 4 cm (1½″) long.
ROLL up into spirals. Brush with beaten egg.
PRESS firmly onto lamb's body.
LET RISE, covered, in warm place, about 20 minutes.
BRUSH with beaten egg.
BAKE on middle oven rack at 180°C (350°F) for 20-30 minutes.
COOL.
SPRINKLE with icing sugar.

Braided Easter Basket

Dough:

2000	g	all-purpose flour	13⅓ cups
2	pkg	**oetker** instant dry yeast	2 pkg.
150	g	sugar	⅔ cup
1	pkg	**oetker** vanilla sugar	1 pkg.
	pinch	salt	pinch
1	btl	**oetker** lemon flavouring concentrate	1 btl.
2		eggs	2
50	g	melted butter or margarine	¼ cup
500	mL	lukewarm milk	2 cups
1		egg, slightly beaten	1

Sugar Glaze:

100	g	icing sugar, sifted	⅔ cup
30-45	mL	hot water	2-3 tbsp.

Method:

PREHEAT oven to 180°C (350°F). Grease a baking sheet and the outside of an ovenproof bowl 17 cm (7″) in diameter.

PREPARE dough using method in basic recipe #351.

DIVIDE dough into 26 equal pieces to form basket. (See illustrations for following steps):

1. WEAVE square with 16 pieces each shaped into 16 cm (6¼″) lengths, starting in middle, working towards outside.

   WRAP around outside of upside-down prepared bowl to form basket.

   CUT off overlapping dough.

2. TWIST two of the pieces together to same size as rim of bowl.

3. PLACE bowl upside down onto prepared baking sheet.

   PLACE the two twisted dough pieces around rim of bowl. Press ends together firmly.

4. SHAPE three pieces of dough (each 40 cm / 16″ long) into a braid. Wrap around a foil paper ring. Brush ends with egg. Press together firmly.

   SHAPE three pieces of dough (each 60 cm / 24″ long) into a braid to form rim of basket. Brush ends with egg. Press together firmly.

   TWIST two long thin pieces of dough together.

   THREAD wire carefully through twisted dough pieces to form handle, leaving wire ends free to attach to basket, when assembling all pieces.

   PLACE all parts onto prepared baking sheet. Brush with beaten egg.

   BAKE on middle oven rack at 180°C (350°F), basket 30-35 minutes, parts 20 minutes. COOL.

Glaze:

COMBINE icing sugar and enough water to make a smooth paste.

ASSEMBLE all parts to form basket, using icing sugar glaze to press parts firmly together.

Brioche Elves

Dough:
Recipe #365

Decoration:

250 g	marzipan	8 oz.
100 g	icing sugar, sifted	⅔ cup
15 mL	cocoa	1 tbsp.
	coloured icing	1

Method:
PREHEAT oven to 220°C (425°F). Grease muffin pan.
PREPARE dough and bake using recipe #365 (brioche muffins).
COOL.
Decoration:
COMBINE marzipan and icing sugar. Mix well into a smooth paste.
COMBINE ⅔ of marzipan mixture with cocoa. Mix well.
ROLL out marzipan-cocoa mixture. Cut out rounds and shape into hats.
ROLL out white marzipan mixture. Shape into beards.
BRUSH marzipan shapes lightly with water. Press tightly onto brioche muffins.
MAKE nose, mouth and eyes with coloured icing or pieces of marzipan.

Apricot Ducks

Dough:

450 g	all-purpose flour	3 cups
1 pkg	**oetker** active dry yeast	1 pkg.
75 g	sugar	⅓ cup
1 pkg	**oetker** vanilla sugar	1 pkg.
pinch	salt	pinch
½ btl	**oetker** lemon flavouring concentrate	½ btl.
4	egg yolks	4
75 g	melted butter or margarine	⅓ cup
250 mL	lukewarm milk	1 cup
1	egg, slightly beaten	1

Decoration:

30-45 mL	strained apricot jam	2-3 tbsp.
	sugar sprinkles	

Method:
PREHEAT oven to 180°C (350°F). Grease and flour a baking sheet.
COMBINE flour and yeast in large bowl. Make a well in centre.
PUT sugar, vanilla sugar, salt, lemon flavouring, egg yolks and melted butter in well.
WORK flour into centre ingredients, gradually adding milk.
KNEAD dough with dough hooks or by hand until blistered and shiny in appearance and no longer sticky, about 5 minutes.
PLACE in greased bowl.
LET RISE, covered, in warm place until doubled in size, about 1 hour.
KNEAD again.
ROLL out dough to about .5 cm (¼") thickness.
CUT out equal number of rounds 8 cm (3"), 4 cm (1½") and 2 cm (¾") in diameter.
USE one round of each size to shape into ducks. (See photo for shaping.)
PLACE onto prepared baking sheet.
LET RISE, covered, about 20 minutes.
BRUSH with beaten egg.
BAKE on middle oven rack at 180°C (350°F) for 15-20 minutes or until golden brown.
BRUSH warm ducks with jam and decorate with sugar sprinkles.

Nut Spiral Cake

Dough:

450 g	all-purpose flour	3 cups	
1 pkg	**oetker** active dry yeast	1 pkg.	
75 g	sugar	⅓ cup	
1 pkg	**oetker** vanilla sugar	1 pkg.	
pinch	salt	pinch	
½ btl	**oetker** lemon flavouring concentrate	½ btl.	
4	egg yolks	4	
75 g	melted butter or margarine	⅓ cup	
250 mL	lukewarm milk	1 cup	

Filling:

100 g	raisins	1 cup
45 mL	rum	3 tbsp.
200 g	ground hazelnuts	2 cups
5 mL	ground cinnamon	1 tsp.
100 g	sugar	½ cup
1 pkg	**oetker** vanilla sugar	1 pkg.
50 mL	milk	¼ cup

Glaze:

50 mL	strained apricot jam	¼ cup

Method:
PREHEAT oven to 180°C (350°F). Grease a 24 cm (9½″) springform pan.
COMBINE flour and yeast in large bowl. Make a well in centre. PUT sugar, vanilla sugar, salt, lemon flavouring, egg yolks and melted butter in well.
WORK flour into centre ingredients, gradually add milk.
KNEAD dough with dough hooks or by hand until blistered and shiny in appearance and no longer sticky, about 5 minutes.
PLACE in greased bowl. LET RISE, covered, in warm place, until doubled in size, about 1 hour. KNEAD again.
ROLL out dough to a 50 cm×50 cm (20″×20″) square.
Filling:
COMBINE all ingredients. Mix well.
SPREAD evenly over dough.
CUT into 5 cm (2″) wide strips.
ROLL up one strip in prepared springform pan. Roll remaining strips loosely around first one, forming a large circle. Press down lightly.
LET RISE, covered, about 30 minutes.
BAKE on lower oven rack at 180°C (350°F) for 35-40 minutes.
SPREAD apricot jam evenly over hot cake.

Marzipan Braids

Dough:

450 g	all-purpose flour	3 cups	
1 pkg	**oetker** active dry yeast	1 pkg.	
75 g	sugar	⅓ cup	
1 pkg	**oetker** vanilla sugar	1 pkg.	
pinch	salt	pinch	
½ btl	**oetker** lemon flavouring concentrate	½ btl.	
4	egg yolks	4	
75 g	melted butter or margarine	⅓ cup	
250 mL	lukewarm milk	1 cup	

Filling:

200 g	marzipan	7 oz.
100 g	ground almonds	1 cup
150 g	sugar	⅔ cup
1 pkg	**oetker** vanilla sugar	1 pkg.
	juice of 1 lemon	

Glaze:

1	egg, slightly beaten	1

Decoration:

30 g	icing sugar, sifted	2 tbsp.

Method:
PREHEAT oven to 190°C (375°F). Grease and flour a baking sheet.
COMBINE flour and yeast in large bowl. Make a well in centre.
PUT sugar, vanilla sugar, salt, lemon flavouring, egg yolks and melted butter in well.
WORK flour into centre ingredients, gradually adding milk.
KNEAD dough with dough hooks or by hand until blistered and shiny in appearance and no longer sticky, about 5 minutes.
PLACE in greased bowl. LET RISE, covered, in warm place, until doubled in size, about 1 hour. KNEAD again.
ROLL out dough to a 50 cm×30 cm (20″×12″) rectangle.
Filling:
COMBINE all ingredients. Mix well.
CUT dough lengthwise into three even pieces.
SPREAD filling evenly over all pieces.
ROLL up each piece, starting at long side.
BRUSH edges with beaten egg. Press together firmly.
BRAID pieces together loosely.
PLACE onto prepared baking sheet. LET RISE, covered, about 20 minutes. Brush with beaten egg. BAKE on middle oven rack at 190°C (375°F) for 25-30 minutes.
COOL.
SPRINKLE with icing sugar before serving.

Blueberry Triangles

Dough:

450 g	all-purpose flour	3	cups
1 pkg	**oetker** active dry yeast	1	pkg.
75 g	sugar	⅓	cup
1 pkg	**oetker** vanilla sugar	1	pkg.
pinch	salt		pinch
½ btl	**oetker** lemon flavouring concentrate	½	btl.
4	egg yolks	4	
75 g	melted butter or margarine	⅓	cup
250 mL	lukewarm milk	1	cup

Filling:

450 g	blueberries	1	lb.

Decoration:

30 g	icing sugar, sifted	¼	cup

Method:
PREHEAT oven to 180°C (350°F). Grease and flour a baking sheet.
COMBINE flour and yeast in large bowl. Make a well in centre.
PUT sugar, vanilla sugar, salt, lemon flavouring, egg yolks and melted butter in well.
WORK flour into centre ingredients, gradually adding milk.
KNEAD dough with dough hooks or by hand until blistered and shiny in appearance, and no longer sticky, about 5 minutes.
PLACE in greased bowl.
LET RISE, covered, in warm place until doubled in size, about 1 hour.
KNEAD again.
ROLL out dough to 1 cm (½″) thickness.
PLACE onto prepared baking sheet.
SPRINKLE blueberries evenly over dough.
LET RISE, covered, about 20 minutes.
BAKE on middle oven rack at 180°C (350°F) for 25-30 minutes.
CUT into triangles or slices.
SPRINKLE with icing sugar just before serving.

Apricot Delights

Dough:

450 g	all-purpose flour	3	cups
1 pkg	**oetker** active dry yeast	1	pkg.
75 g	sugar	⅓	cup
1 pkg	**oetker** vanilla sugar	1	pkg.
pinch	salt		pinch
½ btl	**oetker** lemon flavouring concentrate	½	btl.
4	egg yolks	4	
75 g	melted butter or margarine	⅓	cup
250 mL	lukewarm milk	1	cup
1	egg, slightly beaten	1	

Filling:

500 g	steamed or canned apricot halves	1	lb.
50 g	slivered almonds	½	cup

Method:
PREHEAT oven to 180°C (350°F). Grease a baking sheet.
COMBINE flour and yeast in large mixing bowl. Make a well in centre.
PUT sugar, vanilla sugar, salt, lemon flavouring, egg yolks and melted butter in well.
WORK flour into centre ingredients, gradually adding milk.
KNEAD dough with dough hooks or by hand until blistered and shiny in appearance and no longer sticky, about 5 minutes.
PLACE in greased bowl.
LET RISE, covered, in warm place until doubled in size, about 1 hour.
KNEAD again.
ROLL out dough to 1 cm (½″) thickness.
CUT into 6 cm (2½″) rounds with floured cutter.
BRUSH with beaten egg.
COVER with apricot halves.
SPRINKLE with almonds.
PLACE onto prepared baking sheet.
LET RISE, covered, about 20 minutes.
BAKE on middle oven rack at 180°C (350°F) for 15-20 minutes.

Plum Dumplings

Dough:

450 g	all-purpose flour	3 cups	
1 pkg	**oetker** active dry yeast	1 pkg.	
75 g	sugar	⅓ cup	
1 pkg	**oetker** vanilla sugar	1 pkg.	
pinch	salt	pinch	
½ btl	**oetker** lemon flavouring concentrate	½ btl.	
4	egg yolks	4	
75 g	melted butter or margarine	⅓ cup	
250 mL	lukewarm milk	1 cup	

Filling:

100 g	plum jam	½ cup

Decoration:

150 g	melted butter	¾ cup
	ground poppy seed	
	icing sugar, sifted	

Method:

COMBINE flour and yeast in large mixing bowl. Make a well in centre. PUT sugar, vanilla sugar, salt, lemon flavouring, egg yolks and melted butter in well.
WORK flour into centre ingredients, gradually add milk.
KNEAD dough with dough hooks or by hand until blistered and shiny in appearance, and no longer sticky, about 5 minutes.
PLACE in greased bowl.
LET RISE, covered, in warm place until doubled in size, about 1 hour.
KNEAD again.
SHAPE into a roll.
DIVIDE into 15-20 pieces.
MAKE a deep indentation into each piece.
FILL with plum jam.
PRESS dough together to seal in filling. Shape into round dumplings.
PLACE on a floured cloth.
LET RISE, covered, about 20 minutes.
PLACE into boiling salted water. Cook for 3 minutes on each side.
POUR melted butter over dumplings.
SPRINKLE with mixture of poppy seed and icing sugar.
SERVE hot.

Plum Squares

Dough:

450 g	all-purpose flour	3 cups	
1 pkg	**oetker** active dry yeast	1 pkg.	
75 g	sugar	⅓ cup	
1 pkg	**oetker** vanilla sugar	1 pkg.	
pinch	salt	pinch	
¼ btl	**oetker** lemon flavouring concentrate	½ btl.	
4	egg yolks	4	
75 g	melted butter or margarine	⅓ cup	
250 mL	lukewarm milk	1 cup	

Filling:

approx 100 g	plum jam	½ cup
1	egg, slightly beaten	1

Decoration:

	sugar sprinkles

Method:

PREHEAT oven to 180°C (350°F). Grease and flour a baking sheet.
COMBINE flour and yeast in large bowl. Make a well in centre. PUT sugar, vanilla sugar, salt, lemon flavouring, egg yolks and melted butter in well.
WORK flour into centre ingredients, gradually add milk.
KNEAD dough with dough hooks or by hand until blistered and shiny in appearance and no longer sticky, about 5 minutes.
PLACE in greased bowl.
LET RISE, covered, in warm place, until doubled in size, about 1 hour.
KNEAD again.
(See illustrations)
1. ROLL out dough into squares 10 cm × 10 cm (4″ × 4″) about .5 cm (¼″) thick.
2. CUT a 1 cm (½″) rim without cutting two opposite corners.
3. PLACE some plum jam on inside squares. Cross over rims at cut corners. Press dough firmly together.
PLACE onto prepared baking sheet. LET RISE, covered, about 20 minutes. Brush with beaten egg.
DECORATE with sugar sprinkles.
BAKE on middle oven rack at 180°C (350°F) for 15-20 minutes.

Almond Crescent

Dough:

450 g	all-purpose flour	3	cups
1 pkg	**oetker** active dry yeast	1	pkg.
75 g	sugar	⅓	cup
1 pkg	**oetker** vanilla sugar	1	pkg.
pinch	salt		pinch
½ btl	**oetker** lemon flavouring concentrate	½	btl.
4	egg yolks	4	
75 g	melted butter or margarine	⅓	cup
250 mL	lukewarm milk	1	cup

Filling:

200 g	ground almonds	2	cups
100 g	sugar	½	cup
1 pkg	**oetker** vanilla sugar	1	pkg.
5 mL	ground cinnamon	1	tsp.
50 g	raisins	½	cup
75 mL	hot milk	⅓	cup
30 mL	rum	2	tbsp.

Glaze:

1	egg, slightly beaten	1	

Decoration:

30 g	sliced almonds	⅓	cup

Method:

PREHEAT oven to 180°C (350°F). Grease and flour a baking sheet.

COMBINE flour and yeast in large bowl. Make a well in centre. PUT sugar, vanilla sugar, salt, lemon flavouring, egg yolks and melted butter in well.

WORK flour into centre ingredients, gradually add milk.

KNEAD dough with dough hooks or by hand until blistered and shiny in appearance, and no longer sticky, about 5 minutes.

PLACE in greased bowl. LET RISE, covered, in warm place until doubled in size, about 1 hour. KNEAD again.

ROLL out dough to .5 cm (¼") thick rectangle.

Filling:

COMBINE all ingredients. Mix well.

SPREAD evenly over dough.

ROLL up dough, starting at long side.

SHAPE roll into a crescent on prepared baking sheet.

MAKE incisions at regular intervals into outer rim 3 cm (1") deep.

LET RISE, covered, about 20 minutes.

BRUSH with beaten egg.

SPRINKLE with sliced almonds.

BAKE on middle oven rack at 180°C (350°F) for 25-30 minutes.

Poppy Seed Strudel

Dough:

450 g	all-purpose flour	3	cups
1 pkg	**oetker** active dry yeast	1	pkg.
75 g	sugar	⅓	cup
1 pkg	**oetker** vanilla sugar	1	pkg.
pinch	salt		pinch
½ btl	**oetker** lemon flavouring concentrate	½	btl.
4	egg yolks	4	
75 g	melted butter or margarine	⅓	cup
250 mL	lukewarm milk	1	cup

Filling:

75 mL	milk	⅓	cup
75 g	butter or margarine	⅓	cup
120 g	sugar	⅔	cup
1 pkg	**oetker** vanilla sugar	1	pkg.
6 drops	**oetker** lemon flavouring concentrate	6	drops
200 g	ground poppy seed	1⅓	cups
80 g	raisins	⅔	cup

Glaze:

1	egg, slightly beaten	1	

Method:

PREHEAT oven to 180°C (350°F). Grease and flour a baking sheet.

COMBINE flour and yeast in large mixing bowl. Make a well in centre. PUT sugar, vanilla sugar, salt, lemon flavouring, egg yolks and melted butter in well.

WORK flour into centre ingredients, gradually add milk.

KNEAD dough with dough hooks or by hand until blistered and shiny in appearance and no longer sticky, about 5 minutes.

PLACE in greased bowl. LET RISE, covered, in warm place until doubled in size, about 1 hour. KNEAD again.

ROLL out dough to .5 cm (¼") thick rectangle.

Filling:

COMBINE milk, butter, sugar, vanilla sugar and flavouring in small saucepan. Bring to a boil. Remove from heat.

STIR poppy seeds and raisins into mixture. Mix well.

SPREAD filling evenly over dough.

ROLL up, starting at longer side.

PLACE onto prepared baking sheet.

LET RISE, covered, about 25 minutes.

BRUSH with beaten egg. Pierce several times with fork.

BAKE on middle oven rack at 180°C (350°F) for 25-35 minutes.

Recipe No. 395

Raisin Wheel

Dough:

450 g	all-purpose flour	3 cups	
1 pkg	**oetker** active dry yeast	1 pkg.	
75 g	sugar	⅓ cup	
1 pkg	**oetker** vanilla sugar	1 pkg.	
pinch	salt	pinch	
½ btl	**oetker** lemon flavouring concentrate	½ btl.	
4	egg yolks	4	
75 g	melted butter or margarine	⅓ cup	
250 mL	lukewarm milk	1 cup	

Filling:

150 g	coarse or regular granulated sugar	1 cup	
15 mL	ground cinnamon	1 tbsp.	
150 g	raisins	1¼ cups	

Glaze:

30 mL	milk	2 tbsp.	

Decoration:

icing sugar, sifted

Method:
PREHEAT oven to 180°C (350°F). Grease a 24 cm (9½″) springform pan.
COMBINE flour and yeast in large bowl. Make a well in centre. PUT sugar, vanilla sugar, salt, lemon flavouring, egg yolks and melted butter in well.
WORK flour into centre ingredients, gradually add milk. KNEAD dough with dough hooks or by hand until blistered and shiny in appearance and no longer sticky, about 5 minutes.
PLACE in greased bowl. LET RISE, covered, in warm place until doubled in size, about 1 hour. KNEAD again. ROLL out dough to .5 cm (¼″) thickness.
Filling:
COMBINE sugar, cinnamon and raisins.
SPRINKLE filling evenly over dough.
ROLL up dough starting at longer side. Roll up into a spiral.
PLACE into prepared springform pan.
LET RISE, covered, about 20 minutes.
BRUSH with milk. Pierce surface several times with fork.
BAKE on lower oven rack at 180°C (350°F) for 30-40 minutes. COOL.
SPRINKLE with icing sugar.

Recipe No. 396

Nut Stollen

Dough:

450 g	all-purpose flour	3 cups	
1 pkg	**oetker** active dry yeast	1 pkg.	
75 g	sugar	⅓ cup	
1 pkg	**oetker** vanilla sugar	1 pkg.	
pinch	salt	pinch	
½ btl	**oetker** lemon flavouring concentrate	½ btl.	
4	egg yolks	4	
75 g	melted butter or margarine	⅓ cup	
250 mL	lukewarm milk	1 cup	

Filling:

200 g	ground hazelnuts	2 cups	
150 g	sugar	¾ cup	
1 pkg	**oetker** vanilla sugar	1 pkg.	
2 mL	ground cinnamon	½ tsp.	
½ btl	**oetker** rum flavouring concentrate	½ btl.	
1	egg white, unbeaten	1	

Glaze:

30 mL	milk	2 tbsp.	

Decoration:

icing sugar, sifted

Method:
PREHEAT oven to 180°C (350°F). Grease a 1.5 L (8½″ × 4½″) loaf pan.
COMBINE flour and yeast in large bowl. Make a well in centre. PUT sugar, vanilla sugar, salt, lemon flavouring, egg yolks and melted butter in well.
WORK flour into centre ingredients, gradually add milk. KNEAD dough with dough hooks or by hand until blistered and shiny in appearance, and no longer sticky, about 5 minutes.
PLACE in greased bowl. LET RISE in warm place until doubled in size, about 1 hour. KNEAD again. ROLL out dough to .5 cm (¼″) thickness.
Filling:
COMBINE all ingredients. Mix well.
SPREAD filling evenly over dough.
ROLL up starting from both sides simultaneously so that rolls meet in centre.
PLACE dough into prepared loaf pan.
LET RISE, covered, about 25 minutes.
BRUSH with milk.
PIERCE surface several times with fork.
BAKE on lower oven rack at 180°C (350°F) for 30-40 minutes. COOL.
SPRINKLE with icing sugar.

Apple Turnovers

Dough:

450 g	all-purpose flour	3	cups
1 pkg	**oetker** active dry yeast	1	pkg.
75 g	sugar	⅓	cup
1 pkg	**oetker** vanilla sugar	1	pkg.
pinch	salt		pinch
½ btl	**oetker** lemon flavouring concentrate	½	btl.
4	egg yolks	4	
75 g	melted butter or margarine	⅓	cup
250 mL	lukewarm milk	1	cup

Filling:

300 g	apples	10	oz.
75 mL	white wine	⅓	cup
	juice of 1 lemon		
50 g	sugar	¼	cup
1	cinnamon stick	1	
3	whole cloves	3	
50 g	raisins	½	cup

Glaze:

1	egg, slightly beaten	1	

Decoration:

icing sugar, sifted

Method:

PREHEAT oven to 180°C (350°F). Grease and flour a baking sheet.

COMBINE flour and yeast in large bowl. Make a well in centre.

PUT sugar, vanilla sugar, salt, lemon flavouring, egg yolks and melted butter in well.

WORK flour into centre ingredients, gradually adding milk.

KNEAD dough with dough hooks or by hand until blistered and shiny in appearance and no longer sticky, about 5 minutes.

PLACE in greased bowl.

LET RISE, covered, in warm place until doubled in size, about 1 hour.

KNEAD again.

ROLL out dough to about .5 cm (¼") thickness.

CUT out 10 cm×10 cm (4"×4") squares.

CUT half of squares into strips 1 cm (½") wide without separating outer edges.

Filling:

PEEL and core apples. Cut into small pieces.

COMBINE white wine, lemon juice, sugar, cinnamon stick and cloves. Bring to a boil.

COOK apples in mixture until tender.

DRAIN apples. Remove spices. Add raisins to apples.

SPREAD 15 mL (1 tbsp.) filling on each uncut square.

BRUSH edges with beaten egg.

PLACE cut squares over filling. Press edges together.

PLACE squares onto prepared baking sheet.

LET RISE, covered, about 20 minutes.

BRUSH with beaten egg.

BAKE on middle oven rack at 180°C (350°F) for 18-25 minutes.

COOL.

SPRINKLE with icing sugar.

PUFF

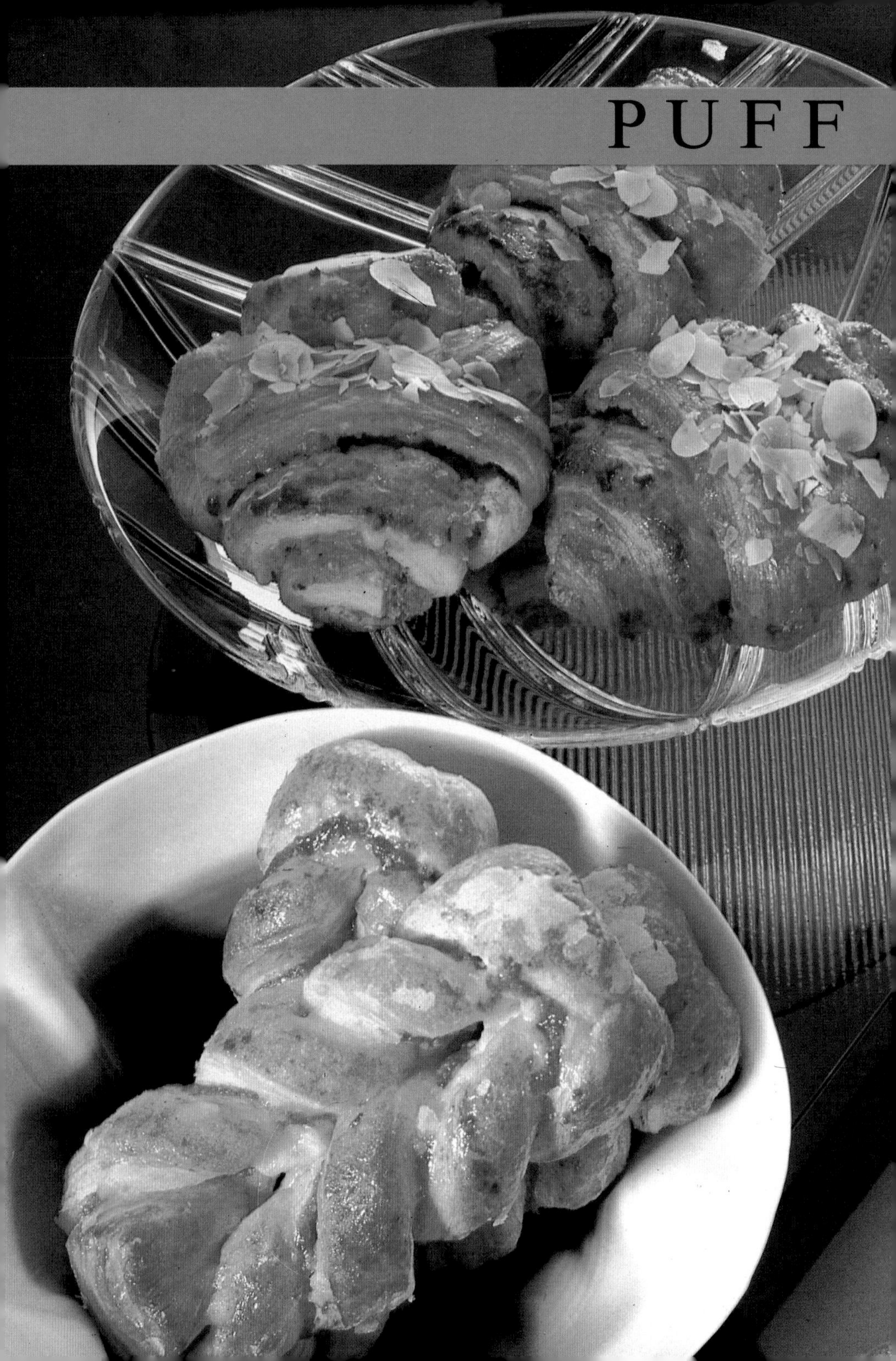

Marzipan Rolls

Dough:
Basic recipe #353

Filling:

100	g	marzipan	3½ oz.
		juice of 1 orange	
25	g	sugar	2 tbsp.
1	pkg	**oetker** natural vanilla sugar	1 pkg.
1		egg white, unbeaten	1
100	g	ground almonds	1 cup

Glaze:

1		egg yolk	1
15	mL	milk	1 tbsp.

Decoration:

20	g	sliced almonds	¼ cup

Method:
PREHEAT oven to 190°C (375°F). Grease and flour a baking sheet.
PREPARE dough using method in basic recipe #353.
ROLL out dough on floured surface to .5 cm (¼″) thickness.
Filling:
COMBINE all ingredients. Mix well.
SPREAD evenly on dough.
DIVIDE dough into two equal halves.
ROLL up, shaping into two rolls.
CUT into slices 5 cm (2″) long. Make a dent in middle with a wooden spoon.
PLACE onto prepared baking sheet.
LET RISE, covered, about 30 minutes.
BRUSH with mixture of egg yolk and milk.
SPRINKLE with sliced almonds.
BAKE on middle oven rack at 190°C (375°F) for 15-20 minutes.

Nut Ties

Dough:
Basic recipe #353

Filling:

200	g	ground walnuts, hazelnuts or almonds	2 cups
75	g	sugar	⅓ cup
1	pkg	**oetker** natural vanilla sugar	1 pkg.
30	mL	rum	2 tbsp.
60	mL	hot milk	¼ cup
1		egg, slightly beaten	1

Glaze:

150	g	icing sugar, sifted	1 cup
15	mL	rum	1 tbsp.
15-30	mL	hot water	1-2 tbsp.

Method:
PREHEAT oven to 190°C (375°F). Grease and flour a baking sheet.
PREPARE dough using method in basic recipe #353.
ROLL out dough on floured surface to .5 cm (¼″) thickness.
Filling:
COMBINE all ingredients except egg. Mix well.
SPREAD evenly on half of dough.
FOLD dough over filling. Press together lightly.
CUT out rectangles 7 cm×10 cm (2¾″×4″).
MAKE a cut lengthwise in middle of each rectangle.
PULL one end through opening.
PLACE dough on prepared baking sheet.
LET RISE, covered, in warm place, about 30 minutes.
BRUSH with beaten egg.
BAKE on middle oven rack at 190°C (375°F) for 15-20 minutes.
Glaze:
COMBINE sifted icing sugar, rum and water to make a smooth paste.
BRUSH evenly onto warm buns.

Recipe No. 400

Pear Tarts

Dough:
Basic recipe #353

Filling:

300 g	steamed or canned pears	10 oz.
50 g	raisins	½ cup
1	egg, slightly beaten	1

Method:
PREHEAT oven to 180°C (350°F). Grease and flour a baking sheet.
PREPARE dough using method in basic recipe #353.
ROLL out dough on floured surface to .5 cm (¼″) thickness.
CUT out rounds with floured cutter 8 cm (3″) in diameter.
Filling:
CUT pears into small pieces.
ADD raisins. Mix well.
PLACE 5 mL (1 tsp.) in centre of half the dough rounds.
BRUSH edges with beaten egg.
CUT out a hole 5 cm (2″) in diameter in remaining dough rounds.
PLACE dough rings onto filling. Press edges firmly together.
MAKE decorations, if desired, out of remaining dough.
BRUSH with beaten egg.
PLACE firmly onto rounds.
PLACE onto prepared baking sheet.
LET RISE, covered, in warm place, about 20 minutes.
BRUSH with beaten egg.
BAKE on middle oven rack at 180°C (350°F) for 15-20 minutes.

Recipe No. 401

Apricot Baskets

Dough:

Basic recipe #353		
1	egg, slightly beaten	1

Filling:
approx

500 g	steamed or canned apricot halves	1 lb.
50 mL	hot apricot jam	¼ cup

Decoration:

20 g	sliced almonds	¼ cup

Method:
PREHEAT oven to 180°C (350°F). Grease and flour a baking sheet.
PREPARE dough using method in basic recipe #353.
ROLL out dough on floured surface to .5 cm (¼″) thickness.
CUT out squares 8 cm×8 cm (3″×3″), using ¾ of dough.
BRUSH with beaten egg.
CUT out strips 1 cm×12 cm (½″×5″) of remaining dough.
PLACE one apricot half onto each square.
COVER crosswise with 2 dough strips.
PLACE onto prepared baking sheet.
LET RISE, covered, in warm place, about 20 minutes.
BRUSH with beaten egg.
BAKE on middle oven rack at 180°C (350°F) for 15-20 minutes.
BRUSH evenly with thin layer of hot apricot jam.
SPRINKLE with sliced almonds.

Poppy Seed Rolls

Dough:
Basic recipe #353

Filling:

150 g	ground poppy seeds	1	cup
100 g	sugar	½	cup
1 pkg	**oetker** vanilla sugar	1	pkg.
5 mL	ground cinnamon	1	tsp.
5 drops	**oetker** lemon flavouring concentrate	5	drops
30 g	dry breadcrumbs	⅓	cup
50 g	raisins	½	cup
15 mL	liquid honey	1	tbsp.
50 g	melted butter or margarine	¼	cup
75 mL	hot milk	⅓	cup
1	egg, slightly beaten	1	

Glaze:

150 g	icing sugar, sifted	1¼	cups
	juice of ½ lemon		
15-30 mL	hot water	1-2	tbsp.

Method:
PREHEAT oven to 180°C (350°F). Grease and flour a baking sheet.
PREPARE dough using method in basic recipe #353.
ROLL out dough on floured surface into a rectangle 25 cm×50 cm (10″×20″).
Filling:
COMBINE all ingredients except egg. Mix well.
SPREAD filling on dough.
ROLL up jelly-roll fashion starting at longer side.
CUT into slices 2 cm (¾″) thick.
PLACE on prepared baking sheet, flatten slightly.
LET RISE, covered, in warm place, about 20 minutes.
BRUSH with beaten egg.
BAKE on middle oven rack at 180°C (350°F) for 18-25 minutes.
Glaze:
COMBINE sifted icing sugar, lemon juice and enough water to make a smooth paste.
SPREAD on poppy seed wheels.

Cream Filled Puffs

Dough:
Basic recipe #353

1	egg, slightly beaten	1	

Filling:

250 mL	whipping cream	1	cup
1 pkg	**oetker** Whip it	1	pkg.
1 pkg	**oetker** natural vanilla sugar	1	pkg.
200 g	fruit, as desired	7	oz.

Decoration:

30 g	icing sugar, sifted	¼	cup

Method:
PREHEAT oven to 180°C (350°F). Grease and flour a baking sheet.
PREPARE dough using method in basic recipe #353.
ROLL out dough on floured surface to .5 cm (¼″) thickness.
CUT out rounds 7 cm (2¾″) in diameter.
PLACE onto prepared baking sheet.
LET RISE, covered, in warm place, about 15 minutes.
BRUSH with beaten egg.
BAKE on middle oven rack at 180°C (350°F) for 15-20 minutes.
Filling:
BEAT whipping cream to soft peaks. Gradually add Whip it and vanilla sugar, beating to stiff peaks.
CUT fruit, as desired.
CUT baked rounds in half horizontally.
SPREAD whipped cream and fruit onto bottom halves.
PLACE tops over filling.
SPRINKLE with icing sugar.

Cherry Turnovers

Dough:
Basic recipe #353

Filling:

50 g	cornstarch	½ cup	
100 g	sugar	½ cup	
75 mL	cherry juice	⅓ cup	
800 g	pitted, steamed or canned cherries	28 oz.	

Glaze:

1	egg, slightly beaten	1	
125 mL	hot apricot jam	½ cup	

Method:
PREHEAT oven to 180°C (350°F). Grease and flour a baking sheet.
PREPARE dough, using method in basic recipe #353.
ROLL out dough on floured surface .5 cm (¼") thickness.
CUT out squares 10 cm×10 cm (4"×4").
Filling:
COMBINE cornstarch, sugar and cherry juice in small saucepan.
ADD cherries. Bring to a boil, stirring constantly, until thickened.
COOL slightly.
BRUSH dough squares with beaten egg.
PLACE cherries in centre of squares.
FOLD opposite corner of dough over to form a pocket. Press firmly together.
BRUSH with beaten egg.
PLACE onto prepared baking sheet.
BAKE on middle oven rack at 180°C (350°F) for 20-25 minutes.
BRUSH hot turnovers evenly with hot apricot jam.

Croissants

Dough:
Basic recipe #353

1	egg yolk	1	
5 mL	milk	1 tsp.	

Method:
PREHEAT oven to 180°C (350°F). Grease and flour a baking sheet.
PREPARE dough using method in basic recipe #353.
ROLL out dough on floured surface to a rectangle 60 cm×30 cm (24"×12").
CUT out squares 15 cm×15 cm (6"×6").
CUT squares into halves, forming triangles.
ROLL up starting at long side.
SHAPE into crescents.
PLACE on prepared baking sheet.
BRUSH with mixture of egg yolk and milk.
BAKE on middle oven rack at 180°C (350°F) for 15-20 minutes.

Blue Cheese Tarts

Dough:
Basic recipe #353

Filling:

250 g	blue cheese	8	oz.
2	eggs	2	
45 mL	sour cream	¼	cup

Decoration:
approx

400 g	steamed or canned pears, sliced	14	oz.

Method:
PREHEAT oven to 220°C (425°F). Grease fluted tart pans.
PREPARE dough using method in basic recipe #353.
ROLL out dough on floured surface to .5 cm (¼") thickness.
CUT out rounds with a floured cutter.
FIT into prepared pans.
PLACE pans on baking sheet.
BAKE on middle oven rack at 220°C (425°F) for 8-10 minutes.
REMOVE tart shells from pans. Let cool.
Filling:
COMBINE all ingredients. Mix well to a smooth consistency.
FILL with cheese mixture.
DECORATE with slice of well drained pear.
PREHEAT oven to 200°C (400°F).
PLACE on greased baking sheet.
BAKE on middle oven rack at 200°C (400°F) for 5-10 minutes.

Camembert Tarts

Dough:
Basic recipe #353

Filling:

250 g	Camembert cheese	8	oz.
2	eggs	2	
50 mL	sour cream	¼	cup

Decoration:

400 g	steamed or cooked apple slices	14	oz.

Method:
PREHEAT oven to 200°C (400°F). Grease fluted tart pans.
PREPARE dough using method in basic recipe #353.
ROLL out dough on floured surface to .5 cm (¼") thickness.
CONTINUE as in recipe #406, replacing blue cheese with Camembert and pears with apples.

Leek Tartlets

Dough:
Basic recipe #353

Filling:

600 g	leeks	21 oz.	
250 mL	sour cream	1 cup	
20 g	all-purpose flour	3 tbsp.	
4	eggs	4	
200 g	grated gruyere cheese	7 oz.	
50 g	grated parmesan cheese	2 oz.	
	salt, pepper, nutmeg, paprika		
50 g	salami, thinly sliced	2 oz.	

Method:
PREHEAT oven to 180°C (350°F). Grease fluted tart pans.
PREPARE dough using method in basic recipe #353.
ROLL out dough on floured surface to .5 cm (¼") thickness.
CUT out rounds with a floured cutter.
FIT into prepared pans.
Filling:
CLEAN leeks. Cut into 2 cm (¾") long pieces.
STEAM in salted water.
DRAIN well.
COMBINE sour cream, flour, eggs and cheeses. Mix well.
ADD salt, pepper, nutmeg and paprika to taste.
PLACE steamed leek onto dough in pans.
SPOON cheese mixture over leek to cover.
PLACE salami pieces on top of cheese mixture.
PLACE pans on baking sheet.
BAKE on middle oven rack at 180°C (350°F) for 18-25 minutes.
REMOVE from pans. Serve hot or cold.

Ham Wheels

Dough:
Basic recipe #353

500 g	sliced ham	1 lb.	
1	egg, slightly beaten	1	

Method:
PREHEAT oven to 180°C (350°F). Grease and flour a baking sheet.
PREPARE dough using method in basic recipe #353.
ROLL out dough on floured surface to .5 cm (¼") thickness.
PLACE ham slices over dough.
ROLL up starting from both sides simultaneously so that rolls meet in centre.
CUT into slices 2 cm (¾") wide.
PLACE onto prepared baking sheet.
BRUSH with beaten egg.
BAKE on middle oven rack at 180°C (350°F) for 15-20 minutes.

Salami Pizza

Dough:
Basic recipe #354

Filling:

30 mL	olive oil	2 tbsp.
500 g	tomatoes, chopped	1 lb.
250 g	mozzarella cheese, grated	8 oz.
200 g	salami, thinly sliced	7 oz.
250 g	asparagus, diced	8 oz.
50 mL	Parmesan cheese, grated	¼ cup
	oregano and basil to	
	taste	
30 mL	olive oil	2 tbsp.

Method:
PREHEAT oven to 225°C (450°F). Grease a baking sheet.
PREPARE dough using method in basic recipe #354.
ROLL out dough thinly on floured surface to form a large circle or 4 small circles.
PINCH up edges.
PLACE on prepared baking sheet.
Filling:
BRUSH dough lightly with olive oil.
DISTRIBUTE tomatoes and then remaining ingredients evenly over dough.
DRIZZLE olive oil over all.
BAKE on middle oven rack at 225°C (450°F) 10 minutes for small or 15-20 minutes for large, or until crust is golden and filling is hot.

Pizza "Deluxe"

Dough:
Basic recipe #354

Filling:

30 mL	olive oil	2 tbsp.
250 g	mushrooms, sliced	8 oz.
20 g	butter	2 tbsp.
	salt and pepper to taste	
1	garlic clove, minced	1
500 g	tomatoes, chopped	1 lb.
250 g	artichoke hearts, diced	8 oz.
50 g	anchovy fillets, finely chopped	2 oz.
15	black olives, halves	15
150 g	salami, thinly sliced	5 oz.
125 g	edam cheese, grated	4 oz.
125 g	gruyere cheese, grated	4 oz.
	oregano and basil to taste	
30 mL	olive oil	2 tbsp.

Method:
PREHEAT oven to 225°C (450°F). Grease a baking sheet.
PREPARE dough using method in basic recipe #354.
ROLL out dough thinly on floured surface to form a large circle or 4 small circles.
PINCH up edges.
PLACE on prepared baking sheet.
Filling:
BRUSH lightly with olive oil.
SAUTÉ mushrooms lightly in butter. Season with salt, pepper and garlic.
DISTRIBUTE tomatoes and then remaining ingredients evenly over dough.
DRIZZLE olive oil over all.
BAKE on middle oven rack at 225°C (450°F) 10 minutes for small or 15-20 minutes for large, or until crust is golden and filling is hot.

Pizza "San Vincenzo"

Dough:
Basic recipe #354

Filling:

30 mL	olive oil	2 tbsp.
500 g	tomatoes, chopped	1 lb.
100 g	mushroom, sliced	3 oz.
100 g	artichoke hearts, diced	3 oz.
15 mL	capers	1 tbsp.
100 g	anchovy fillets, finely chopped	3 oz.
15	black olives, sliced	15
375 g	mozzarella cheese, grated	12 oz.
	salt, pepper, basil and oregano to taste	
30 mL	olive oil	2 tbsp.

Method:
PREHEAT oven to 225°C (450°F). Grease a baking sheet.
PREPARE dough using method in basic recipe #354.
ROLL out dough thinly on floured surface to form a large circle or 4 small circles.
PINCH up edges.
PLACE on prepared baking sheet.
Filling:
BRUSH lightly with olive oil.
DISTRIBUTE tomatoes and then remaining ingredients evenly over dough.
DRIZZLE olive oil over all.
BAKE on middle oven rack at 225°C (450°F) 10 minutes for small or 15-20 minutes for large, or until crust is golden and filling is hot.

Vegetable Pizza

Dough:
Basic recipe #354

Filling:

30 mL	olive oil	2 tbsp.
500 g	tomatoes, chopped	1 lb.
20 g	butter	2 tbsp.
300 g	spinach, chopped	10 oz.
150 g	mushrooms, sliced	5 oz.
2	garlic cloves, minced	2
100 g	artichokes, sliced	3 oz.
250 g	gouda cheese, grated	8 oz.
	oregano, salt and pepper to taste	
30 mL	olive oil	2 tbsp.

Method:
PREHEAT oven to 225°C (450°F). Grease a baking sheet.
PREPARE dough using method in basic recipe #354.
ROLL out dough thinly on floured surface to form a large circle or 4 small circles.
PINCH up edges.
PLACE on prepared baking sheet.
Filling:
BRUSH lightly with olive oil.
DISTRIBUTE tomatoes evenly over dough.
SAUTÉ spinach, mushrooms and garlic in butter until tender.
DISTRIBUTE evenly over tomatoes.
PLACE artichokes and cheese evenly over mixture.
SEASON with oregano, salt and pepper.
DRIZZLE olive oil over all.
BAKE on middle oven rack at 225°C (450°F) 10 minutes for small or 15-20 minutes for large, or until crust is golden and filling is hot.

Ham Snacks

Dough:

500 g	all-purpose flour	3⅓	cups
1 pkg	**oetker** instant dry yeast	1	pkg.
2 mL	salt	½	tsp.
2 mL	ground caraway	½	tsp.
50 g	melted butter or margarine	¼	cup
250 mL	lukewarm milk	1	cup

Filling:

250 g	cubed ham	8	oz.
30 mL	chopped parsley	2	tbsp.
	salt and pepper to taste		
1	egg yolk	1	
5 mL	milk	1	tsp.
	coarse salt		

Method:

PREHEAT oven to 200°C (400°F). Grease and flour a baking sheet.
PREPARE dough, using method in basic recipe #351.
ROLL out dough on floured surface.
CUT into squares 12 cm × 12 cm (5" × 5").
Filling:
COMBINE ham, parsley and seasonings. Mix well.
CUT squares into halves to form triangles.
PLACE ham mixture evenly onto dough.
ROLL up from long side.
PLACE onto prepared baking sheet.
BRUSH with mixture of egg yolk and milk.
SPRINKLE with salt.
BAKE on middle oven rack at 200°C (400°F) for 15-20 minutes.

Shrimp Toast

4 slices	toast bread (see recipe #425)	4	slices

Filling:

500 g	herb cream cheese	1	lb.
125 g	shrimps, cooked	4	oz.
	watercress		

Garnish:

	lemon slices

Method:

TOAST bread on both sides.
SPREAD cream cheese evenly over slices.
COVER with shrimps and watercress.
GARNISH with lemon slices.

Onion Treat

Dough:

300 g	all-purpose flour	2	cups
1 pkg	**oetker** instant dry yeast	1	pkg.
5 mL	salt	1	tsp.
15 mL	sugar	1	tbsp.
50 g	melted butter or margarine	¼	cup
approx 125 mL	lukewarm milk	½	cup

Filling:

1000 g	onions, finely chopped	2	lbs.
50 g	butter or margarine	¼	cup
500 mL	sour cream	2	cups
30 mL	cornstarch	2	tbsp.
3	eggs, slightly beaten	3	
	salt, pepper, caraway		
125 g	diced bacon, partially cooked	4	oz.

Method:

PREHEAT oven to 200°C (400°F). Grease a baking sheet.
PREPARE dough using method in basic recipe #351.
ROLL out dough to .5 cm (¼") thickness.
PLACE onto prepared baking sheet.
Filling:
SAUTÉ onions in butter until tender.
COMBINE sour cream, cornstarch and eggs. Mix well.
SEASON to taste with salt, pepper and caraway.
ADD onions.
SPREAD mixture evenly over dough.
SPRINKLE with bacon.
LET RISE, covered, in warm place, about 30 minutes.
BAKE on middle oven rack at 200°C (400°F) for 20-25 minutes.

Pork Dumplings

Dough:

250 g	all-purpose flour	1⅔	cups
1 pkg	**oetker** instant dry yeast	1	pkg.
	salt		
1	egg	1	
50 g	shortening	¼	cup
approx 125 mL	lukewarm milk	½	cup
200 g	potatoes, cooked, peeled and mashed	7	oz.

Filling:

30 mL	shortening	2	tbsp.
150 g	onions, finely chopped	5	oz.
250 g	smoked pork, cubed	8	oz.
30 mL	parsley, chopped	2	tbsp.
	salt and pepper to taste		

For deep frying:

oil or shortening

Method:

PREPARE dough using method in basic recipe #351.
WORK potatoes into dough.
ROLL out dough on floured surface to .5 cm (¼") thickness.
CUT out rounds 8 cm (3") in diameter.
Filling:
SAUTÉ onions and smoked pork in shortening until golden.
SEASON with parsley, salt and pepper.
COOL.
PLACE 5 mL (1 tsp.) pork mixture onto each dough round.
FOLD dough over, shaping into a ball. Press edges together firmly.
HEAT fat to 190°C (375°F). Keep at an even temperature.
FRY dumplings, a few at a time, until golden brown on both sides.
REMOVE from fat. Drain well on paper towelling.
SERVE hot.

Gourmet Steak Treats

Ingredients:

4 slices	rye toast bread (recipe #424) butter or margarine	4 slices	

Filling:

500 g	mushrooms, sliced	1 lb.	
50 g	butter or margarine salt and pepper to taste	¼ cup	
50 mL	parsley, finely chopped	¼ cup	
4	steak fillets (about 150 g/5 oz. each) hot paprika	4	
30 mL	olive oil salt	2 tbsp.	

Parsley butter:

100 g	butter, softened	½ cup	
1	garlic clove, minced	1	
15 mL	finely chopped parsley	1 tbsp.	

Method:
TOAST bread on both sides.
SAUTÉ mushrooms in butter.
SEASON with salt, pepper and parsley.
SEASON steaks with paprika.
HEAT oil.
BROWN steaks on both sides to desired doneness.
Parsley butter:
COMBINE all ingredients. Mix well.
PLACE mixture in decorating bag with star tube.
SQUEEZE one shape per serving.
CHILL.
RESERVE extra for another use.
PLACE steaks, mushrooms and parsley butter rosette on toast slices.
SERVE hot.

Italian Toast

Ingredients:

4 slices	rye toast bread (recipe #424) butter or margarine	4 slices	

Filling:

4 slices	mortadella	4 slices	
250 g	mushrooms, sliced and sautéed salt and pepper to taste	8 oz.	
1	garlic clove, minced	1	
15 mL	finely chopped parsley	1 tbsp.	
2	tomatoes, sliced	2	
4 slices	tilsit, havarti or Swiss cheese	4 slices	

Method:
PREHEAT oven to 220°C (425°F).
TOAST bread on both sides.
SPREAD butter evenly over slices.
COVER with mortadella.
SEASON mushrooms with salt, pepper, garlic and parsley.
DISTRIBUTE evenly over mortadella.
COVER with tomato and cheese slices.
BAKE on middle oven rack at 220°C (425°F) for 5-8 minutes, or until heated through.

Ham and Pear Toast

Ingredients:

4 slices	toast bread (recipe #425) butter or margarine	4 slices

Filling:

4 slices	cooked ham	4 slices
4	pear halves, steamed or canned, sliced	4
4 slices	Swiss cheese	4 slices
50 mL	lingonberry jam or red currant jelly	¼ cup

Method:
PREHEAT oven to 220°C (425°F).
TOAST bread on both sides.
SPREAD butter evenly over slices.
COVER with ham, pear slices and cheese.
BAKE on middle oven rack at 220°C (425°F) for about 5-8 minutes, or until heated through.
SERVE warm with jam.

Ham and Asparagus Toast

Ingredients:

4 slices	toast bread (recipe #425) butter or margarine	4 slices

Filling:

4 slices	cooked ham	4 slices
398 mL can	asparagus spears	14 oz. can
4 slices	brick, mozzarella or Swiss cheese	4 slices

Method:
PREHEAT oven to 220°C (425°F).
TOAST bread on both sides.
SPREAD butter evenly over slices.
COVER with ham, asparagus and cheese.
BAKE on middle oven rack at 220°C (425°F) for about 5-8 minutes, or until heated through.

Linseed Bread

Dough:

400 g	dark rye flour	2	cups
150 g	whole wheat flour	1	cup
50 g	linseeds or flax seeds	¼	cup
1 pkg	**oetker** instant dry yeast	1	pkg.
10 mL	salt	2	tsp.
5 mL	coriander	1	tsp.
5 mL	anise seed	1	tsp.
2 mL	fennel	½	tsp.
approx			
375 mL	lukewarm water	1½	cups
	linseeds or flax seeds		

Method:
PREHEAT oven to 190°C (375°F). Grease and flour a baking sheet.
PREPARE dough, using method in basic recipe #351.
LET dough rise 1 hour.
SHAPE into a loaf.
PLACE onto prepared baking sheet.
MAKE diagonal slashes with sharp knife 1 cm (½")
deep on top of loaf.
BRUSH loaf with water.
SPRINKLE with linseeds.
LET RISE, covered, in warm place, about 45 minutes.
BAKE on middle oven rack at 190°C (375°F) for
20-25 minutes.

Oatmeal Bread

Dough:

225-		1½-	
265 g	all-purpose flour	1¾	cups
350 g	whole wheat flour	2⅓	cups
50 g	oats	⅓	cup
1 pkg	**oetker** instant dry yeast	1	pkg.
15 g	sugar	1	tbsp.
10 mL	salt	2	tsp.
approx			
375 mL	lukewarm water	1½	cups
30 mL	melted butter or margarine	2	tbsp.
	oats		

Method:
PREHEAT oven to 190°C (375°F). Grease and flour a baking sheet.
PREPARE dough using method in basic recipe #351.
Use just enough flour to make a soft dough.
LET dough rise 45 minutes.
SHAPE into an oval loaf.
PLACE onto prepared baking sheet.
MAKE crosswise indentations with sharp knife about
1 cm (½") deep.
BRUSH with water.
SPRINKLE with oats.
LET RISE, covered, in warm place, about
20 minutes.
BAKE on middle oven rack at 190°C (375°F) for
20-25 minutes.

Rye Toast Bread

Dough:

340- 375	g	all-purpose flour	2¼- 2½	cups
200	g	rye flour	1⅓	cups
1	pkg	**oetker** instant dry yeast	1	pkg.
5	mL	salt	1	tsp.
30	mL	melted butter or margarine	2	tbsp.
375	mL	lukewarm water	1½	cups

Method:
PREHEAT oven to 190°C (375°F). Grease a 1.5 L (8½″ ×4½″) loaf pan.
PREPARE dough using method in basic recipe #351. Use just enough flour to make a soft dough.
LET dough rise 45 minutes.
PLACE dough into prepared loaf pan.
LET RISE, covered, in warm place, about 30 minutes.
BAKE on lower oven rack at 190°C (375°F) for 30-35 minutes.

Toast Bread

Dough:

500	g	all-purpose flour	3⅓	cups
1	pkg	**oetker** instant dry yeast	1	pkg.
5	mL	salt	1	tsp.
15	mL	sugar	1	tbsp.
30	mL	melted butter or margarine	2	tbsp.
300	mL	lukewarm water	1¼	cups

Method:
PREHEAT oven to 190°C (375°F). Grease a 1.5 L (8½″ ×4½″) loaf pan.
PREPARE dough using method in basic recipe #351.
LET dough rise 30 minutes.
PLACE dough into prepared loaf pan.
LET RISE, covered, in warm place, about 20 minutes.
BAKE on lower oven rack at 190°C (375°F) for 26-40 minutes.

Cracked Wheat Herb Bread

Dough:

250 g	whole wheat flour	1⅔ cups	
200 g	light rye flour	1⅓ cups	
50 g	cracked wheat	⅓ cup	
1 pkg	**oetker** instant dry yeast	1 pkg.	
10 mL	salt	2 tsp.	
30 mL	dried parsley flakes	2 tbsp.	
15 mL	dried herbs, mixed	1 tbsp.	
	(chives, dill, chervil,		
	tarragon, basil)		
approx			
300 mL	lukewarm water	1¼ cups	

Method:
PREHEAT oven to 190°C (375°F). Grease and flour a baking sheet.
PREPARE dough, using method in basic recipe #351.
LET dough rise 1 hour.
SHAPE into a round loaf.
MAKE a hole in centre of loaf, forming a ring.
PLACE dough on prepared baking sheet.
MAKE slashes with sharp knife about 1 cm (½″) deep on top of loaf.
LET RISE, covered, in warm place, about 1 hour.
BAKE on middle oven rack at 190°C (375°F) for 40-45 minutes.

Caraway Bread

Dough:

500 g	whole wheat flour	3⅓ cups	
1 pkg	**oetker** instant dry yeast	1 pkg.	
10 mL	salt	2 tsp.	
15 mL	caraway seeds	1 tbsp.	
approx			
300 mL	lukewarm water	1¼ cups	
50 g	bacon, cooked and diced	2 oz.	
	all-purpose flour		

Method:
PREHEAT oven to 190°C (375°F). Grease and flour a baking sheet.
PREPARE dough using method in basic recipe #351.
LET dough rise 45 minutes.
SHAPE into a round loaf.
PLACE dough onto prepared baking sheet.
MAKE slashes with sharp knife about 1 cm (½″) deep on top of loaf.
LET RISE, covered, in warm place, about 25 minutes.
BRUSH with water.
SPRINKLE with flour.
BAKE on middle oven rack at 190°C (375°F) for 25-30 minutes.

Baguettes

Dough:

1000 g	all-purpose flour	6⅔	cups
2 pkg	**oetker** instant dry yeast	2	pkg.
15 mL	salt	1	tbsp.
approx			
675 mL	lukewarm water	2½	cups

Glaze:

1	egg, slightly beaten	1	

Method:

PREHEAT oven to 190°C (375°F). Grease and flour a baking sheet.
PREPARE dough, using method in basic recipe #351.
LET dough rise 45 minutes.
DIVIDE into 4 portions. Shape each into a long thin baguette.
PLACE dough onto prepared baking sheet.
MAKE diagonal slashes with sharp knife 1 cm (½″) deep on top of each baguette.
LET RISE, covered, in warm place, about 20 minutes.
BRUSH with beaten egg.
BAKE on middle oven rack at 190°C (375°F) for 15-20 minutes.

Poppy Seed Buns

Dough:

500 g	all-purpose flour	3¼	cups
1 pkg	**oetker** instant dry yeast	1	pkg.
5 mL	salt	1	tsp.
pinch	ground pepper		pinch
pinch	ground nutmeg		pinch
1	egg	1	
30 g	melted butter or margarine	2	tbsp.
approx			
250 mL	lukewarm milk	1	cup

Decoration:

1	egg, slightly beaten poppy seeds	1	

Method:

PREHEAT oven to 190°C (375°F). Grease and flour a baking sheet.
PREPARE dough using method in basic recipe #351.
LET dough rise 45 minutes.
DIVIDE dough into 12 portions about 50 g (2 oz) each.
SHAPE into round balls.
MAKE slashes crosswise with sharp knife 1 cm (½″) deep on top of rolls.
PLACE onto prepared baking sheet.
LET RISE, covered, in warm place, about 20 minutes.
BRUSH with beaten egg.
SPRINKLE with poppy seeds.
BAKE on middle oven rack at 190°C (375°F) for 15-20 minutes.

Potato Raisin Bread

Dough:

500	g	all-purpose flour	3⅓ cups
1	pkg	**oetker** instant dry yeast	1 pkg.
pinch		salt	pinch
75	g	sugar	⅓ cup
1		egg	1
½	btl	**oetker** lemon flavouring concentrate	½ btl.
50	g	melted butter or margarine	¼ cup
250	mL	lukewarm milk	1 cup
300	g	cooked, mashed potatoes, cold	1½ cups
100	g	raisins	1 cup

Glaze:

1		egg, slightly beaten	1

Method:

PREHEAT oven to 190°C (375°F). Grease two 1.5 L (8½ × 4½″) loaf pans.
PREPARE dough using method in basic recipe #351.
ADD potatoes to dough when mixing.
KNEAD raisins into dough.
LET dough rise 1 hour.
DIVIDE dough into 2 portions.
SHAPE each into a loaf and place in prepared pans.
LET RISE, covered, in warm place, about 50 minutes.
BRUSH with beaten egg.
BAKE on lower oven rack at 190°C (375°F) for 30-35 minutes, or until golden brown.

Farmer's Bread

Dough:

250	g	whole wheat flour	1⅔ cups
250	g	light rye flour	1⅔ cups
1	pkg	**oetker** instant dry yeast	1 pkg.
10	mL	salt	2 tsp.
15	mL	caraway seeds	1 tbsp.
10	mL	coriander	2 tsp.
5	mL	fennel seeds	1 tsp.
30	mL	olive oil	2 tbsp.
approx 300	mL	lukewarm water	1¼ cups

Method:

PREHEAT oven to 200°C (400°F). Grease and flour a baking sheet.
PREPARE dough using method in basic recipe #351.
LET dough rise 1 hour.
SHAPE into a round loaf.
PLACE loaf onto prepared baking sheet.
MAKE diamond shape slashes with sharp knife 1 cm (½″) deep on top of loaf (see illustration).
LET RISE, covered, in warm place, about 40 minutes.
BAKE on middle oven rack at 200°C (400°F) for 25-30 minutes.

Nut Bread

Dough:

250 g	all-purpose flour	1⅔	cups
250 g	whole wheat flour	1⅔	cups
1 pkg	**oetker** instant dry yeast	1	pkg.
10 mL	salt	2	tsp.
15 mL	sugar	1	tbsp.
30 mL	oil	2	tbsp.
375 mL	lukewarm milk	1½	cups
120 g	chopped hazelnuts	1	cup

Method:
PREHEAT oven to 190°C (375°F). Grease and flour a baking sheet.
PREPARE dough using method in basic recipe #351.
ADD hazelnuts to dough. Knead well.
LET dough rise 1 hour.
SHAPE into a loaf.
PLACE onto prepared baking sheet.
MARK lengthwise slashes with sharp knife 1 cm (½") deep on top of loaf.
LET RISE, covered, in warm place, about 40 minutes.
BAKE on middle oven rack at 190°C (375°F) for 25-30 minutes.

Sesame Loaf

Dough:

500 g	all-purpose flour	3⅓	cups
1 pkg	**oetker** instant dry yeast	1	pkg.
15 mL	sugar	1	tbsp.
10 mL	salt	2	tsp.
	grated rind of 1 orange		
1	egg	1	
approx			
250 mL	lukewarm water	1	cup
30 mL	melted butter or margarine	2	tbsp.

Decoration:

30 g	sesame seeds	2	tbsp.

Method:
PREHEAT oven to 190°C (375°F). Grease and flour a baking sheet.
PREPARE dough using method in basic recipe #351.
LET dough rise 45 minutes.
SHAPE into a loaf.
BRUSH loaf with water.
SPRINKLE evenly with sesame seeds.
PLACE loaf onto prepared baking sheet.
MAKE several holes on top of dough 2 cm (¾") deep.
LET RISE, covered, in warm place, about 20 minutes.
BAKE on middle oven rack at 190°C (375°F) for 20-25 minutes.

Notes